ADVANCE PRAISE FOR
THE POWER OF EYE CONTACT

"Drawing on everything from Darwin to dating tips, neuro-psychology to salsa dancing, *The Power of Eye Contact* paints an enlightening picture of how our eyes evolved into our most important communication devices, and how understanding them makes life better in nearly every arena. This book should be required reading for everyone who plans on finding true confidence, healthy relationships, and a thriving career."

—Jaimal Yogis, author of *Saltwater Buddha*

"Something magical happens when two people connect eye to eye. Michael Ellsberg's wonderful book helps you create that magic every day."

—Marci Shimoff, author of *New York Times* bestseller *Happy for No Reason*

"Effective business networking depends on effective eye contact. If you want to improve your networking skills, this book will be an important read."

—Dr. Ivan Misner, author of the *New York Times* bestselling *Masters of Networking* and *Truth or Delusion?*

"Ellsberg takes us on a captivating journey through the world of eye contact. Both mysterious and rewarding, the text reveals the powerful secrets of using the eyes to connect with others."

—Rom Brafman, coauthor of the *New York Times* bestseller *Sway*

"Rumi often speaks of the soul mystery that gets exchanged through the eyes, in the glance. Michael Ellsberg provides a clear guide on how we can bring this practice, with all its beauty and power, into our own lives."

—Coleman Barks, author of *The Essential Rumi,*
The Soul of Rumi, and *Rumi: The Book of Love*

"The Power of Eye Contact is a must-read book if you want a lasting relationship—or want to deepen the one you're in. Few skills hold as much potential in the realm of the heart as offering your deep presence through your gaze. Michael Ellsberg shows you the way."

—Marie Forleo, author of *Make Every Man Want You*
(or Make Yours Want You More)

"I use eye contact in my own fighting as a way of making sure my opponent knows I mean business. *The Power of Eye Contact* offers great guidance for using eye contact to project calm and confidence in hostile, competitive, or dangerous situations. I recommend it for anyone interested in competitive sports, self-defense, and martial arts."

—Urijah Faber, world champion mixed martial artist

"After I swam the Amazon, demand for my public speaking skyrocketed. No one has taught me more about connecting with audiences on a visceral level than Michael Ellsberg."

—Martin Strel, holder of four Guinness World Records in distance swimming, coauthor of *The Man Who Swam the Amazon*

"Michael Ellsberg incisively surveys the many centuries of literature on the qualities of eye contact, skillfully interviews contemporaries who shed light on its complex dynamics, and with a clear eye and open heart offers profoundly practical guidance to those who hunger to see deeper—into others and themselves."

—Thomas Farber, author of *The Beholder*

Jessica Agullo

About the Author

Michael Ellsberg is the founder of Eye Gazing Parties (www.eyegazingparties.com), the world's first singles event based on eye contact. Eye Gazing Parties have occurred on several continents now and have been covered by the *New York Times*, CNN, *Good Morning America*, and in major media outlets around the globe. *Elle* magazine (UK) called Eye Gazing Parties "New York's hottest dating trend."

Prior to this book, he collaborated with Dr. Marc Gerstein on *Flirting With Disaster: Why Accidents Are Rarely Accidental*, which was published by Union Square Press in June 2008 and reviewed in the *Wall Street Journal*.

Michael was born in San Francisco in 1977, grew up in Berkeley, and graduated from Brown University in 1999, Phi Beta Kappa and magna cum laude.

He lives in Brooklyn with his fiancée, Jena la Flamme.

Visit Michael on the web at www.ellsberg.com.

The Power of
Eye Contact

The Power of Eye Contact

Your Secret for Success in Business, Love, and Life

Michael Ellsberg

HARPER

NEW YORK · LONDON · TORONTO · SYDNEY

HARPER

HarperCollins books may be purchased for educational, business,
or sales promotional use. For information please write: Special Markets
Department, HarperCollins Publishers, 10 East 53rd Street,
New York, NY 10022.

FIRST EDITION

Designed by Mia Risberg

Library of Congress Cataloging-in-Publication Data
is available upon request.

ISBN 978-0-06-178221-3

10 11 12 13 14   OV/RRD   10 9 8 7 6 5 4 3

For Jena

May I gaze into your eyes forever

. . . los ojos . . . mudas lenguas de amorios.

(. . . the eyes, silent tongues of love.)

—MIGUEL DE CERVANTES, from *Don Quijote*[1]

Contents

A Note to Readers

I welcome your comments, questions, critiques, feedback, corrections, stories, experiences, and anecdotes. Please write to me at michael@powerofeyecontact.com. I won't answer everything personally, but I will read it all and will answer the most interesting questions and queries.

I may also post your questions, stories, or anecdotes on the book's blog, www.powerofeyecontact.com/blog. So when you write, let me know if you're OK with that, and if so, how you'd like me to identify and credit you (name, website, etc.).

I have put many free downloadable bonuses to this book on www.powerofeyecontact.com/bonus, including a free teleseminar series covering the topics of this book, audio interviews with experts, my free ebooks "How to Host an Eye Gazing Party" and "Beauty Secrets for Better Eye Contact" (that roar of clicking sounds you hear around you is the onslaught of straight male readers rushing to download that last title), and a free subscription to my "Power of Eye Contact" newsletter with stories, tips, insights, updates and event invitations.

In writing this book, I was often asked, "Is the importance of direct eye contact universal, or does it apply only in some cultures and not others?"

There's no question in my mind that norms around eye contact must shift from culture to culture. However, I decided not to delve into the topic of eye contact and culture in this book; it seemed too easy to slip into overgeneralization and stereotype. Instead, I have written the book from the perspective of the world I know, attitudes and norms prevalent in the urban northeast and west coast of the United States. For more thoughts on this topic, see the endnotes.[1]

A note on interviews: Over the course of eight months researching and writing this book, I conducted more than three dozen interviews with scientists, psychologists, public speakers, business people, dating coaches, sales professionals, fighters, athletes, spiritual teachers, and others who generously shared their time and their insight into eye contact. My understanding of the topic was immeasurably deepened thanks to their contributions.

Oftentimes, I felt that interviewees' thoughts and words were more interesting coming straight from them—allowing their own unique personalities and voices to shine through—as opposed to my own paraphrasing. Thus, I frequently chose to present their words directly in interview format. I mark these passages clearly with last names to indicate who was speaking.

I have edited all interviews for space, clarity, and flow while preserving the essential content and voice of the speaker.

MICHAEL ELLSBERG
NEW YORK, NY
JUNE 2009

Introduction

Let's imagine a game.

You will be asked a series of questions about the personal and professional life of a person you have not met or even seen: Is she happy? Sad? Does she enjoy her job? How are her family relations? Is she in love? Is she energized by life? Beaten down?

To base your answers on something other than sheer guess, you will be given a clue: You will be allowed to observe one body part (or pair of body parts) of this person, in real life, for five minutes.

Which body part would you choose? The feet? The hands? The nose? The mouth?

The answer, I think, is obvious. Most of us would choose the eyes.

"[T]he mirror of the mind is the face, its index the eyes," Cicero tells us in the first century B.C.[1] For thousands of years, from high literature to proverbs and folk wisdom, and in spiritual traditions around the world, the eyes have held special significance as the "windows of the soul."

"The eye is the lamp of the body; so then if your eye is clear, your whole body will be full of light. But if your eye is bad, your whole body will be full of darkness. If then the light that is in you is darkness, how great is the darkness!" the Bible tells us.[2]

Saint Jerome, presaging the Moral Majority by over 1,500 years, warns women of good morals: "Avoid the company of young men. Let long haired youths dandified and wanton never be seen under your roof. Repel a singer as you would some bane." So that they may avoid such temptations, Jerome warns women to play their emotional cards close to their chest: "The face is the mirror of the mind and a woman's eyes without a word betray the secrets of her heart."[3]

If the eyes offer a direct line to our desires, emotions, and feelings, then when two eyes meet, the fireworks of human connection begin. "A lover's eyes will gaze an eagle blind," writes Shakespeare.[4] "Words are only painted fire; a look is fire itself," says Mark Twain.[5] "[W]hat is it that you express in your eyes? It seems to me more than all the words I have read in my life," writes Whitman.[6] "The eyes of men converse as much as their tongues, with the advantage that the ocular dialect needs no dictionary, but is understood all the world over," Ralph Waldo Emerson tells us.[7]

These last three quotes above are quite remarkable. Three of the greatest stylists in the history of language—Twain, Whitman, and Emerson—are all telling us essentially the same thing: Their chosen medium of artistic self-expression, the written word, is impotent next to the power of the gaze.

Have you ever said "I want to be able to look him in the eyes and tell him . . ."? Implicit in this phrase is the idea that we cannot tell a lie when we are looking someone in the eyes; whatever our mouths say, we believe that our eyes will tell the truth.

What is it about the eyes and the gaze that holds such power for us? Why do they reveal such depth about our inner world? And what is it about direct eye contact that we find so meaningful—and so potentially terrifying?

In this book, we are going to go on a journey into a rich, captivating, and sometimes mysterious topic. We will talk with a diverse, merry, and cantankerous crew of people who have thought a lot about this subject, including scientists, poets, spiritual teachers, sales professionals, a legendary sports coach, fighting champions, professional public speakers, psychologists, dating experts, a pickup artist, and even a *Playboy* centerfold included for good measure. They will all help us unlock the mystery of our eyes and of eye contact.

But make no mistake: the aim of this book is neither theoretical nor poetic. The ultimate aim of this book is to help us lead better lives—to get more of what we want from life by mastering the power of eye contact. If you can imagine an area of life that is important to you and that involves relating to other humans face to face, then eye contact is a crucial part of it.

Yet it is possible to botch eye contact. It can be done very, very poorly. Or not at all. It can be done in a way that repels rather than attracts. Eye contact can go wrong in many ways. There is a good chance you are making some of these mistakes right now, without knowing it. In fact, some of your social interactions may not be going as well as you'd hoped because of it.

I know this, because I used to be *awful* at eye contact. Not just awful, but scared and terrified of it.

That was before I learned the secrets presented in this book. The good news is that it's not that hard to become really good at eye contact. People now tell me all the time that they feel safe, comfortable, appreciated, respected, understood—and even sometimes energized—when met by my gaze.

I wasn't born this way. (Actually, maybe I was—all babies are natural eye contact pros, as we'll soon see. But we lose this facility quickly as self-consciousness develops.) I *learned* how to have this quality of eye contact.

I learned all of this over years. But I've put all of what I've learned over these years of experience, observation, and research into this book. Now you can learn in a matter of *weeks* what took me years to master. I know because I've seen friends, family members, and readers transformed by the lessons and examples contained herein.

While there is a lively trade in books on body language—and many of them, including some cited here, are excellent—there has never been a book that dives in depth and exclusively *into* the social and business aspects of this most important, intriguing, spiritually rich, and scientifically studied aspect of body language: eye contact. Never, until now.

You hold in your hands a book with the power to change your life dramatically within a short period of time.

This book is your concise guide to harnessing the potent force of eye contact for success in your work and personal relationships. It teaches you how to stop being "eye shy" and start being "eye *bold*." It teaches you how to build and maintain powerful eye contact in all your relationships and interactions.

Master this art with the help of this book, and you will instantly begin to notice three things:

- You will start meeting more people right away.
- Your connections with the people you already know will deepen.
- You will feel, look, and act more confident.

It is no exaggeration to say that mastering the art of effective eye contact could be one of the most impactful things you ever do in a short amount of time.

Who Am I and How Did I Get So Interested in Eye Contact?

I was born in San Francisco in 1977. In 2005, living in New York City, I was single, as I had been for most of my twenties. Like many single twenty-somethings, I would frequently go out to bars and clubs, hoping that—amidst the thumping music and stolen glances over furtive sips of alcohol—I would find my match.

Instead, what I found was small talk. Lots of it.

"Where are you from?"

"What do you do for a living?"

"What neighborhood do you live in?"

"Do you like living in New York?"

Blah, blah, blah.

I started calling this "résumé talk." It felt more like a job interview than a prelude to a life of passion.

At the end of one night, I realized I had been in five different conversations that had all contained some permutation on these résumé questions.

Now, I'm all in favor knowing where someone is from, and what he or she does for a living. But will this stuff really spark intense attraction in anyone at the outset? Is this the stuff fairy tales are made of?

There's got to be a more interesting way to meet people, I thought.

I had been an avid salsa dancer for over a decade, and around the same time as my disappointing bar experiences I began to notice that the dances that were most intense for me were the ones with the most—and best—eye contact.

A dancing partner could be the queen of technique, the rock star of fancy turns. She could have hips with more swivel than an Aeron office chair, and curves more treacherous than the Pacific Coast Highway, but if her eye contact was dead—or worse, and more commonly, nonexistent—the dance would also feel dead.

By contrast, a woman could be rather plain on the outside. She could have a modest repertoire of turns and an undeveloped sense of the music. But if the quality of her eye contact was good—inviting, deep, soulful, expressive, steady, grounded, joyful—the dance would invariably be a pleasure. And when a woman who really knew how to move *also* had good eye contact, forget it—the result was *electrifying*, creating a sense of excitement and connection so powerful I wished the song would stretch to eternity.

There was not one dance going on, I realized, but two: the dance between bodies in motion, and the dance between the eyes. The former was the foundation. The latter was the electrical connection.

This experience with eye contact in my salsa dance—in combination with another stunning experience I had involving eye contact and dating, which I recount in Chapter 4—inspired a vision in my mind: get a bunch of singles together to stop the mindless chatter and start the gaze. Instantly, I saw it in my mind: thirty or forty singles together, in a room, sharing this same electricity I experienced in that gaze on the salsa dance floor, accessible to all, not just dancers.

The words "Eye Gazing Parties" came to my mind.

I explained my vision to a bar owner in the East Village, and he liked the idea of twenty or thirty drink-hungry singles coming into his place on an off night.

I immediately wrote up some initial copy and breathlessly sent it out to my friends in New York:

The eyes are the windows to the soul, so it's a lot easier to have a mesmerizing conversation with someone after you've spent three minutes looking into his or her eyes. That is the simple idea behind Eye Gazing Parties. Banal chitchat about employment status, the location of your apartment, or where you're from is not a great way to spark a captivating connection with an alluring new person. Eye contact is.

Here's how it works. An even number of singles gets together in an attractive space. After meeting over drinks and jazz, the group splits into pairs, and each pair spends three minutes looking at each other's eyes, no talking, with inviting beats in the background. The pairs switch up every three minutes, for a total of forty-five minutes. Then there's a party afterwards, with drinks flowing and luscious beats vibing. The eye gazing has an electrifying effect on the party. Simply put, three minutes of eye contact is the Cadillac of icebreakers. Come try out the exciting new way to meet single souls!

To my knowledge, the first event in the world in which strangers congregated in a bar with the express intent of peering into one another's eyes occurred on December 7, 2005. Twenty-three people showed up, mostly friends and friends of friends.

By a fluke, the *New York Times* got wind of the event and sent a reporter. A few weeks later, a small piece about the event appeared in the Sunday "City" section. After that, the calls started rolling in. CNN, *Good Morning America*, the Associated Press, German national radio, Brazilian national television, the BBC, *Elle* magazine—they all covered subsequent Eye Gazing Parties. Without setting out to be one, I became an "expert source" for the media about eye contact when most reporters started asking me, "What is it about eye contact that makes it so powerful?"

At first, I had little authority to answer these questions beyond my own limited experience and the fact that other people in the media seemed to think I was an authority. But as the Eye Gazing Parties developed I became more and more interested in eye contact beyond the parties. I began reading everything I could on it. I began talking to experts: both formal experts, such as academic scholars, and street-smart experts— people who use eye contact skills with fantastic success every day in their line of work, from sales professionals and public speakers to members of law enforcement to "seduction gurus" who charge exorbitant sums teaching men how to pick up women in bars. Through my Eye Gazing Parties, I've also had the privilege of observing and participating in more intense, direct eye contact than anyone else I know of.

In this book, my aim is to share with you all I've learned over these years so that your life can be lit up and energized by the same quality of eye contact and connection that I've been lucky enough to enjoy.

The Power of
Eye Contact

ONE

What Bill Clinton Knows About Eye Contact

The Evolution of Rapport

I have a friend who has always *despised* Bill Clinton," a person at a cocktail party told me during the time I was writing this book. "In fact, he had level of hatred for the man that reached epic proportions. It was almost a personal hatred. Yet, somehow my friend found himself at a function which Bill Clinton was attending. And, within the swirl of the crowd, he was introduced to Clinton.

"In that moment, face to face, all of my friend's personal animosity toward Clinton disappeared, in one instant," my new acquaintance at the party continued. "As they were shaking hands, Clinton made eye contact with my friend in a way so powerful and intimate, my friend felt as though *the two of them were the only people in the room.* Everyone else and everything else melted away, and it was just them standing there shaking hands, for a second."

While writing this book I heard some version of this story about Clinton not once but *three times*. Either this is some kind of urban legend about his aura of charisma, or he really did have something special going on with his eyes. Hearing a story like this from three different people, I decided to Google "Bill Clinton" and "eye contact." Several references to Clinton's eye powers turned up.

A *New York Times Magazine* profile near the beginning of his presidency referred to his facility for "making eye contact so deep that recipients sometimes seem mesmerized. Tabloid rumors aside, Clinton embodies the parallels between the seductions of politics and the seductions of sex. As one Clinton watcher said recently: 'It's not that Clinton seduces women. It's that he seduces everyone.'"[1]

A post on the celebrity news blog WENN said, "Actress Gillian Anderson has discovered the secret behind former U.S. President Bill Clinton's sex appeal—lingering eye contact."

Anderson (Special Agent Dana Scully on *The X-Files*) spoke on *Late Night with David Letterman* of an encounter she'd had with Clinton several years earlier: "We all, mostly women, lined up. And when he gets to you, he takes your hand and makes eye contact. After he leaves and he moves on to the next person, he looks back at you and seals the deal. When I got home, I expected to have a message from him, and I didn't. I bet women across America expect it too."[2]

The reason I tell this story is not to make a political point. (For those who smell partisanship, I should point out that Ronald Reagan was famous for having similar powers of face-to-face charm, although I couldn't find any specific references to the quality of his eye contact.) Rather, I point it out to draw attention to a phrase that comes up again and again when someone is skilled at eye contact: *When he looked at me, I felt like we were the only people in the room.*

This, friends, is the power of eye contact: the ability to forge a connection so strong between humans, in so short a time, that two people feel like one in an instant. I know of no other force in human experience that can work such magic so quickly.

Can you think of all the different contexts in which it would be helpful to forge fast, quick, and strong feelings of connectedness, commonality, and trust with others?

Dating, sales, meetings, public speaking and business presentations, job interviews, a heart-to-heart with your family or loved ones, a romantic night alone with your sweetie—these are only a few areas that stand to benefit from practiced eye contact. We'll explore how eye contact relates to all these realms in subsequent chapters.

Effective eye contact can be the difference between excelling in social interactions and failing. It can help land you a job. It can help land you a date. It can help deepen your connection with the people you love. It can make or break work-group cooperation and cohesion. Simply put, eye contact is one of the most powerful forces in human face-to-face interaction.

Women, imagine the words "Will you marry me?" coming from the mouth of just the right man . . . on a romantic beach . . . with a big sparkly rock of a diamond ring held for your grasp . . . while the man's eyes are staring straight into your . . . *feet!*

Relevant in boxing, writing, reading

The Power of Attention in a World Gone ADD

Why is eye contact so central to feelings of connection and trust?

Toward the end of my time writing this book, I had the privilege of speaking to Dr. Paul Ekman, professor emeritus of psychology at the University of California, San Francisco.

Ekman is universally acknowledged as the leading authority on the expression of emotion through the face. He is the author of dozens of books and scholarly articles on the subject, and he has been named by the American Psychological Association as one of the most influential psychologists of the twentieth century. Most recently, he coauthored *Emotional Awareness: Overcoming the Obstacles to Psychological Balance and Compassion* with the Dalai Lama.

Ekman is famous for having put to rest the argument—most notably put forward by Margaret Mead—that facial expressions are culturally arbitrary. In the late sixties, he traveled to Papua New Guinea. He showed remote tribesmen, who had never spent time with Westerners before, pictures of Westerners with various facial expressions, such as happiness or sadness. Through an interpreter, he told various mini-stories, along the lines of "This woman's baby was just killed," or "This man sees a good friend," and asked the tribesmen to pick out which expression best illustrated the story. The tribesmen easily and quickly picked out the expressions that you and I would pick out as well.

ELLSBERG: I've talked with all kinds of practitioners, from sales people to dating experts to public speakers, who tell me that eye contact is crucial to what they do. Why do so many people feel passionately that eye contact is important in face-to-face interaction?

EKMAN: If you're not looking at me at least part of the time while I'm talking to you, I don't think you're listening to me. People don't talk unless people give them signals that they're listening. They can do it with "Yeah, mm-hmm's," or head nods, or by looking at them at the end of a phonemic clause. I used to tell my students, "Try with a friend in a conversation to give them no listener responses—no vocal ones, no facial ones, no head nods—see what happens." Within ten seconds, the other person says, "Is something wrong? Are you listening?" People won't talk without these cues.

I had thought that there would be an elaborate evolutionary answer to my question—particularly coming from a man well-known for his theories about the evolutionary roots of body language.

But it turns out his answer is much simpler: Eye contact signals attention. If you're looking at my eyes, it signals to me that you're paying attention. If you're not, it signals you're not paying attention.

Twitter, Facebook, instant messaging, text messaging, cell phones, BlackBerries—we are living in a world where no one, it seems, has attention for anyone or anything for more than a few moments.

How rare it is when someone pays attention to us. Think, even, of that phrase *pay attention.* In industrialized nations, at least, attention is becoming almost as scarce a resource as money. Someone who pays it to you is giving you something of true value. No wonder we respond well when people make eye contact with us. It suggests that they are listening, that they are present to us, that they are taking us in. It suggests that they care about us.

Attention matters, particularly in this ADD age, and I know of no signal more powerful than eye contact to show that you are giving someone your complete attention and presence.

Eye Contact on the Savannah: The Evolution of the Gaze

We've seen that eye contact derives at least some of its power because it is a good barometer of the level, focus, and quality of our *attention.* Our eyes reveal our focus.

Yet the eyes reveal a world of information beyond just the focus of our attention. Think of all the emotions—happiness, anger, sadness, surprise, fear—that can be detected loud and clear from a simple glance at someone's eyes (or, more accurately, the facial muscles around the eyes, which create various expressions). When we make eye contact with another person, we are in some sense giving that person keys to our emotional world. Whatever we're feeling, the other person is likely to get at least a gut level sense of our state of mind.

Think, for a moment, how strange and remarkable this is. We usually think of emotions as something deeply private and personal. Yet in our evolution, not only did we develop the emotions themselves, we also developed a mechanism for broadcasting them to the world—a "neural wifi," as psychologist Daniel Goleman puts it[3]—so that all those around us can pick up on them.

Have you ever been at a party, observed someone make an entrance, and gotten an instant "read" on that person? "Confident," "shy," "nervous," "outgoing," "happy." That person was unconsciously, unintentionally, and nonlinguistically communicating his or her inner state to you.

Why would this constant "neural wifi" have evolved? One might think that the opposite might be more likely to evolve. Think of all the situations in which you might like to conceal your true feelings about something. Asking that attractive co-worker out for dinner, for example, when inside you're pins and needles. Asking for a raise, a sale, or a job confidently, when inside you know that if the answer is "no," you might not be able to make your mortgage or rent payment next month. Speaking calmly to a crowd, when inside you'd rather crawl into a hole and hide. Playing a round of poker when your cards are garbage.

We all know that hiding our true feelings in situations like these is difficult indeed (though certainly not impossible, as we'll see in Chapter 8, "Truth and Eyes"). Given the lengths we often go to conceal these true feelings, why would we have evolved the capacity to communicate our interior states to others automatically and involuntarily via body language?

I asked Frans de Waal this very question. De Waal is one of the best-known primatologists in the world, a professor of primate behavior at Emory University, and the author of *Our Inner Ape: A Leading Primatologist Explains Why We Are Who We Are* and *Chimpanzee Politics: Power and Sex Among Apes.*

ELLSBERG: From a purely self-interested perspective, there would seem to be an advantage in being able to hide our emotions and express them only when we choose to. Why did we evolve such a system for making our emotions so apparent to others?

DE WAAL: What you suggest would be true if we were purely competitive. The assumption in the social sciences, law, and economics is that we are put on this world to compete with others and get the best out of our dealings with others—a manipulative type of human.

But we actually evolved to be highly cooperative, like many animals. And humans even more so than many animals. We have highly cooperative societies.

Let's say, for example, you have the choice of going hunting with Friend A or Friend B. Friend A is an emotional character who displays all his emotions—so you know exactly what you're getting with that person. Friend B is inscrutable, and you can never tell what he thinks or feels, and he will never tell you. Which one are you going to hunt with? With your friends, you want to have the whole array of emotions displayed.

———————

Paul Ekman offered me an explanation of the evolution of body language similar to de Waal's.

EKMAN: There are two branches to contemporary evolutionary theory. One is individual selection and one is group selection. Group selection has been very unpopular in the past thirty years. But even people like E. O. Wilson are recognizing that it was a mistake to say that things were selected *only* if they help my genes, and not if they help the whole social group.

The presumption has to be that, more often than not, for *you* to know how *I* feel is useful to *me* and to the social group. We know that the nature of our ancestral environment for 95 percent of the time—which was when nature did its work—was to foster cooperation among small groups. You couldn't deal with predators and prey without group effort.

————————

In our ancestral environment, it appears, there was a very high premium on conveying accurate, instantaneous communication about the internal state of our co–tribe members. This value applied as much to the *giver* of the information as to the *receiver.* If your co-tribesman was surprised by a snake in the path, angry at an intruder, fearful of an alligator tail he just saw, or anxious about being lost, it would help *both* of you survive if you were able to pick up instantly on his or her interior state and adjust your plan of action accordingly.

Not surprisingly, the emotions that are most quickly and readily detected in the face and eyes are fear, anger, and surprise, Ekman told me.

EKMAN: Fear has the greatest exposure of sclera, the white area that surrounds the iris. Surprise has some but not as much. The big eye signals are in fear, anger, and surprise.

Most of the information we get from the eyes comes from changes in the aperture, which is what you see of the iris and the sclera—the white—as a result of muscle action in the lower eyelid and the upper eyelid. There are four muscles on each side of the face that change that aperture. That's where the information is.

In anger, we have a "glare," where the upper eyelid is raised and the brow is lowered, that puts pressure on the upper eyelid, and the lower eyelid is tense. You get a glaring look. It's a very powerful anger signal. You don't need to see anything on the rest of the face, although often it's accompanied by congruent facial movements.

Happiness has some eye signals, but not as forcefully. I've distinguished what I call the "Duchenne" smile in honor of the French neurologist who first made this observation, which I proved one hundred years later. The true smile of enjoyment, what I have called the "Duchenne smile," involves movement of a muscle around the eye—orbicularis oculi, pars lateralis—which causes the eye coverfold to move down very slightly. Crow's-feet wrinkles or cheek movement—I can produce that with a big, broad phony smile. But as Duchenne said, that muscle "doesn't obey the will." Most people can't move it voluntarily. "And its absence unmasks the false friend."

Here's a very interesting thing. It must not have been useful, over the course of our evolution, for other members of our species to know whether we were really enjoying ourselves or just acting as if we were.

We can distinguish it through very careful measurement. We can teach people to be right about 75 percent of the time. So it's not a signal. People can distinguish anger, fear, and surprise much much more easily, even at a great distance.

ELLSBERG: Fear, anger, and surprise—those are emotions, one can imagine in our past, on which it would be very useful to get an instant read. You're out with a hunting partner, and you see a look of fear on his face. You know instantly that something is not right, and you get ready for action.

EKMAN: That's right. And if you see a look of anger, you know *you* might be in trouble. This is the 200th anniversary of Darwin's birth and the 150th anniversary of the publication of *On the Origin of Species*, and the evidence is as close to conclusive as evidence ever gets, that Darwin was right and Mead was wrong: there are six or seven emotions that have a universal expression.[4] The role of the eyes—or the muscles around the eyes, to be precise—is the same, regardless of culture. That's part of our biology, shaped by our ancestors.

Darwin on Body Language

Imagine that a man butts in line in front of you at an airport. He is runty and small, and as you point out to him that there's a line, he turns around and says, "Piss off. I'll stand here if I want. And if you've got a problem with it, I'll slug you, *pow*, right in the kisser!"

You've got a good foot of height on this man, and you don't find him a serious threat at all. In fact, you find his threat as laughable as it is unbelievable. You're determined not to let this guy get away with such behavior and words toward you.

Now, picture your posture as you respond to this man. Imagine yourself in one of the following two stances. Go ahead: stand up and actually put yourself in the physical positions I describe. Ask yourself: is it more likely that you respond in:

Stance A: Standing tall and straight, with chest forward and shoulder down, elbows slightly out and forearms in with knuckles out, facing the man squarely, with narrow eyes; or

Stance B: Slightly crooked, humpbacked posture, with shoulders up and forward, elbows in and arms out, palms facing up to the sky, with head crooked to the side slightly and eyes wide open.

Which position do you see yourself adopting in this situation?

I imagine that most readers picked Stance A. This stance, also known as "standing tall and straight," is the universal expression of readiness, preparedness, and confidence in the face of a challenge. It communicates that you're not going to put up with such treatment and that the other person better back down, *or else*.

Yet, when I say a stance "communicates" one thing or another, what do I actually mean? When we think of communication, we usually think of words, either spoken or written. How is it possible that our *bodies,* including our posture and our *eyes*, communicate reliable information to others? And furthermore, we also usually think of communication as intentional. How often have you just started babbling random words unintentionally? (At least, how often while sober?) How does all this unintentional body and eye communication actually work?

In 1872, thirteen years after he reached the height of international fame with *On the Origin of Species*, Darwin wrote a book called *The Expression of the Emotions in Man and Animals*. Though not nearly as widely read as *Origin* and *The Descent of Man*, it is an accessible, fascinating work, and it remains a foundational document in understanding the development of body language in humans and other animals.

In this book, Darwin outlines three principles, which—he suggests—explain the majority of body language. The first two of these he calls the principle of "serviceable expressions" and the principle of "antithesis."[5]

According to his principle of serviceable expressions, some body movements and expressions arise as an instinctual result of strong emotion; they either help relieve the feelings or help the individual prepare for actions that are likely to occur in conjunction with the emotion. One example which—as we will see—cuts to the heart of this book is the attitude of confidence, and related feelings such as resolve, determination, decisiveness, and preparedness.

From Darwin's perspective of "serviceable" gestures, the fact that Stance A is the posture of resolve, not Stance B, makes perfect sense. If you might have to push or elbow or punch someone, you want your chest out, your elbows and knuckles out, and your shoulders down, ready for movement. You want to be standing tall, at least before blows begin, appearing as large and dominant as possible. You want your gaze focused on your opponent, both to filter out all else but the threat in front of you and to project the idea "I mean business."

In turn, Stance B—with the crooked, off-balance body, the arms and fists in—puts you in a poor position to initiate or defend against a blow, and it also makes your body appear smaller, connoting less of a threat.

Our ancestors who reflexively carried their bodies in Stance A when ready to defend themselves successfully protected themselves more often, and passed on more of their genes, than those who exhibited Stance B in preparation for fighting.

All of this amounts to a plausible explanation of the utility of standing tall as an expression of confidence. Yet, we are left with a puzzling question. Stance B, also commonly called a "shrug," is also a universal expression, one of resignation, when we lack confidence or conviction that we can do anything to resolve a situation. What possible useful function would the components of shrugging—raised shoulders, inward elbows, upward palms, raised eyebrows, and wide eyes—have as an expression of helplessness and doubt?

It is here that Darwin's second principle, "antithesis," comes into play. Darwin says that an "indignant man, who resents, and will not submit to some injury" adopts a stance like "A" above, with straight frame, shoulders straight ahead, puffed chest, and fists ready for action, with primed arm and leg muscles, narrowed eyes, and a stiff jaw. However, he says:

> *The helpless man unconsciously . . . raises his eyebrows; at the same time he relaxes the muscles about the mouth, so that the lower jaw drops. The antithesis is complete in every detail, not only in the movements of the features, but in the positions of the limbs and in the attitude of the whole body . . .* [6]

In other words, raising the shoulders, turning the elbows in and the palms up, cocking the head, raising the eyebrows, and opening the eyes and the mouth serve absolutely no utilitarian function in relation to the attitude of resignation and helplessness (indeed, it is hard to imagine what a utilitarian function in relation to these attitudes would even be). But, because they are the exact opposite of how we appear when we are confident, resolved, and determined, we use the shrug to express the opposite of these attitudes.

I got a plentiful taste of this expression when traveling to Cuba in 2000, with a license from the U.S. Treasury Department allowing me and other Americans to visit the island to donate medicine to people in need.

Under Cuba's socialist system, it is very difficult to get a raise in one's job or to get fired. This provides neither a carrot nor a stick as incentive to provide good service in places like restaurants and airline counters.

On my return, the Cuban government decided it was going to use the Cubana airliner I was scheduled to fly on to transport Cuban athletes to the Summer Olympics instead. The result was an airplane-load of people stranded on the island for two extra days, many without adequate cash or even a way to call or e-mail home to alert family members.

As you can imagine, most of us were frantic, trying to secure courtesies from the airline such as a place to sleep and cash to buy food.

You have never seen so much shrugging on the part of the airline and airport staff. Practically every other body motion was a shrug. All of this communicated the message loud and clear, without words: "I don't care." "I can't help you." "I'm not going to do anything about it." "Look elsewhere for help." "Don't blame *me*." (Of course, I did find it hard to blame them, as they weren't going to get paid any better if they did provide good service, and they weren't going to get disciplined or be held accountable if they didn't.)

From all these examples, we can see that body language communicates to us in two ways: the direct way and the indirect way, which correlate roughly to Darwin's two principles mentioned above: serviceable expressions and antithesis. In the direct way, a certain expression or posture has a direct utility in relation to the emotion involved by preparing us for action related to that emotion (such as fighting, in relation to anger or resolve).

In indirect communication, the posture has no particular utility in relation to the emotion (such as shrugging in relation to resignation). But, because the body movements involved in a shrug are directly opposed to those we display when we are feeling confident, a shrug conveys a lot of information instantaneously, and it appears that evolution selected us to transmit this body communication involuntarily.

So what does all of this have to do with the eyes? In *The Expression of the Emotions,* Darwin talks about eye expressions extensively and shows how they evolved according to the same rules of "serviceable expressions" and "antithesis" we've been talking about in relation to body language in general.

We know intuitively that rage is one of the most instantly recognizable emotions through the eyes, and Ekman confirmed that for us as well. What is going on with the eyes during rage? Heart rate and respiration go up, filling the extremities with blood to be ready for action. This also results in a rush of blood to the head ("hotheaded," "blowing your top," "red-faced with rage," etc.). The effect of all this on the eyes, Darwin points out, is a perfect example of a serviceable expression:

> The eyes are always bright, or may, as Homer expressed it, glisten with rage. They are sometimes bloodshot, and are said to protrude from their sockets—the result, no doubt, of the head being gorged with blood, as shown by the veins being distended.[7]

Throughout the book, Darwin gives dozens of examples of eye expressions that result both as a serviceable expression (i.e., as a result of some physiological reaction that bears a utilitarian function in relation to the emotion being experienced) and as an antithesis expression (which bears no useful function, yet, by the contrast, communicates volumes), as we saw in the rolled eyes of the shrug.

Hands down and lashes up, there is no more varied, nuanced, clear, and versatile communicator of emotion than our eyes—or, more accurately, the set of muscles around the eyes. No other body area comes even remotely close. When people say "the eyes are the window to the soul," what they really mean is that the eyes are the window to our emotional states.

Think of all the emotions and attitudes that are regularly communicated instantaneously with the eyes: fear, surprise, anger, love, like, joy, anxiety, hatred, disgust, agreement, disagreement. If you can feel it, your eyes can show it.

This is why eye contact is such a potent force in human face-to-face interaction and connection. By looking at someone's eyes, and allowing the other person to simultaneously look at yours, all walls keeping you out of each other's interior emotional lives come tumbling down, and you instantly let each other in on what is going on inside of you, for better or for worse.

There is some question as to what it means, exactly, to say that your "eyes" communicate emotion. Do the eyeballs themselves actually communicate emotion? Or is all this emotion communicated exclusively by the facial muscles immediately around the eyes?

In *Body Language*, one of the best-selling books on body language of all time, Julius Fast comes down very strong on one side of this question: "Far from being windows of the soul, the eyes are physiological dead ends, simply organs of sight and no more, differently colored in different people to be sure, but never really capable of expressing emotions in themselves. . . . [T]he emotional impact of the eyes occurs because of their use and the use of the face around them."[8]

There's no doubt that the use of the eyes (darting around or steady, looking askance or directly) and the facial muscles around the eyes communicate volumes. We've already heard Paul Ekman on the importance of the facial muscles around the eyes. As for the direction of gaze, Frans de Waal suggested to me that the whites of the eyes developed precisely to highlight these shifts in gaze: "The eye is already important for many primates, and we humans with our whites around our eyes have enhanced that. By putting whites around the iris, the direction of movement becomes even more conspicuous."[9]

But several examples I share below show that Fast's notion that the eyeballs themselves are "physiological dead ends," expressing nothing in and of themselves, is clearly false.

The *eyeballs* themselves—or at least their exterior—communicate a lot of information about our emotional lives, particularly through their state on the spectrum from dullness to brightness.

"Bright eyed and bushy tailed," "twinkle in his eye," "starry-eyed." These are all expressions that indicate excitement, vitality, and happiness; the latter even has a connotation of *too much* excitement, a naïve, puppyish enthusiasm, such as that displayed by a pubescent girl upon spotting a boy-band heartthrob.

It is obvious, to me at least, that happier people have shinier eyes. In fact, it is one of the primary ways I can tell if people *are* happy, and one of the primary things that I myself find attractive in women. One of the first things I noticed about my fiancée, Jena, on our first date, was the shine in her eyes. They were as sparkly as Christmas lights and tinsel.

I'm not talking about color here; I'm talking about the luster and brilliance of whatever color a person's eyes happen to be. I'm a salsa dancer, and in a Latin club, you end up dancing with a lot of people with black hair and brown eyes. Believe me, when a dancer is happy, the darkest brown eyes (which can even appear jet black in a nightclub) can shine like a strobe light in the dark club.

I am not the only one who has noticed this correlation between happiness and sparkling eyes. None other than Darwin noticed it, and he gave an explanation for it:

A bright and sparkling eye is as characteristic of a pleased or amused state of mind, as is the retraction of the corners of the mouth and upper lip. . . . Their brightness seems to be chiefly due to their tenseness, owing to the contraction of the orbicular muscles and to the pressure of the raised cheeks. But, according to Dr. Piderit . . . the tenseness may be largely attributed to the eyeballs becoming filled with blood and other fluids, from the acceleration of the circulation, consequent on the excitement of pleasure. . . . Any cause which lowers the circulation deadens the eye. I remember seeing a man utterly prostrated by prolonged and severe exertion during a very hot day, and a bystander compared his eyes to those of boiled codfish.[10]

One of the most beautiful descriptions I've seen of the difference between vibrant and dead eyes comes from a young spiritual writer named Sera Beak, in her book *The Red Book: A Deliciously Unorthodox Approach to Igniting Your Divine Spark:*

You know those people you meet whose eyes are sort of vacant and lifeless? Those who are just slumping along life's crowded highways, not ever really reaching deeper into their soul's pockets? What about the opposite type, those whose eyes dance and beam and cry and flash? The ones who seem to glow, despite their imperfections, who tend to attract good friends and good happenings like a magnet, who seem to beam out a calm and fearless sense of self?[11]

I experienced my own version of Darwin's codfish-eyes anecdote once while talking with a woman at a party. I had struck up a conversation with her, and soon into the conversation, it was clear that she was very unhappy about her life. Why was she unhappy? She hated her job. What was her job? She was a stripper. She hated the customers. She hated her boss. She hated having to hide her work from family members (which was perhaps why she was griping to a complete stranger instead).

Sure, I noticed this woman's remarkably protuberant physique while talking with her, as most straight men probably did. But another thing I noticed—and in fact what struck me most about her—was the complete deadness in her eyes. Rather than reflect light, they seemed almost to absorb it, like spiritual black holes. The whites were more like off-whites.

We made eye contact as we talked. But as I looked at her I

didn't feel any spirit look back at me, just blankness. I recalled a line from Gertrude Stein, on Stein's native Oakland, California: "There's no *there* there." No one was home. This woman's eyes communicated almost nothing, and by so doing, communicated everything about the sad condition she was in.

I happen to have female friends who strip and actually enjoy it, so I don't want this anecdote to be taken as a tirade against the profession of stripping. But it was clear that this young woman was not enjoying it, and it showed loud and clear in her eyes. "Anyone who has ever looked into the glazed eyes of a soldier dying on the battlefield will think hard before starting a war," Otto von Bismarck said, observing the phenomenon in yet another context.[12] The poor man flattened by exhaustion in Darwin's example, the sad stripper, and the dying soldier all exhibit what we often call "glassy eyes" or "eyes glazed over." When we say a person's "eyes glazed over from boredom," we typically mean that the eyes have become dull and expressionless, roughly the same as "glassy eyes."

I have pondered quite a bit why this phenomenon is called "glassy" or "glazed." The essential quality of this state seems to be dullness in the eyes. Yet, glaze and glass both have connotations of shininess. Remember putting glaze on mugs in pottery class? And glass too has connotations of shininess and reflection—a glassy ocean, as surfers call it, refers to the time in the evening after the wind has died down and the ocean is smooth and shiny, exploding with the colors of the sunset above. Why would we call dull eyes glazed or glassy, when in almost every other context it refers to shininess?

I believe these references actually exhibit a great deal of subtlety about the expressiveness of the eyes; on some intuitive level, these words make sense. Seeing an eye glazed over, or glassy, you feel as though there is an extra layer in between you and the person inside. While that outside barrier might be slightly shiny, there is no depth at all—not the deep, radiant oceans of reflection on an eye we call "sparkly" or "shiny."

Gaga Eyed in the Crib

In his book *Blink: The Power of Thinking Without Thinking*, which anyone interested in body language should read, Malcolm Gladwell refers to our capacity to infer the emotional states of others intuitively as "mind reading." According to Gladwell, mind reading via people's expressions is a crucial and automatic skill to navigate the social world:

> *Every waking minute that we are in the presence of someone, we come up with a constant stream of predictions and inferences about what that person is thinking and feeling. When someone says "I love you," we look into that person's eyes to judge his or her sincerity. . . . If you were to approach a one-year-old child who sits playing on the floor and do something a little bit puzzling, such as cupping your hands over hers, the child would immediately look into your eyes. Why? Because what you have done requires explanation, and the child knows she can find an answer on your face.*[13]

Gladwell's example of babies and eye contact highlights that we don't need to look to such extremes as tiger attacks and snake scares in our distant evolutionary history to see the value of reading and giving off instant emotional clues *sans* language. When you and I were babies, we had a lot of things that were very useful for us to communicate, and for our mothers to understand, with eyes and vocalizations—"I want milk!" "There's something lodged in my throat!" "I love you"—long before we developed our capacity for language, or even any conscious understanding of what milk, throats, or love were.

Both Ekman and de Waal stressed the need for mother–infant communication as another driver of the evolution of body language.

EKMAN: I'll give you another, totally independent reason why these facial signals evolved. Mothers would not be able to deal with their infants, and become attached to them, and be motivated to put up with the shit—literally—if it wasn't for the googling and giggling and laughing, and also knowing when the infant is frustrated, sad, in pain, etc.

De Waal offered a similar explanation:

DE WAAL: Of course, body language starts between mother and child. We are mammals, and since mammals are dependent on their mothers, they better let her know when they're hungry and cold and so forth. It starts with those relationships where there's an immediate need, and a high survival value for displaying whether you need food or not. I argue in my writings that empathy evolved because females needed to respond to the needs of their offspring. That's the basis of all of this.

Eye Contact and Social Intelligence

We've seen how eyes communicate volumes about our emotional states, and we've seen why this capacity to transmit our emotional lives evolved in our past. Yet, how does eye contact actually work, on a neurological, physiological level? What goes on in our brains when one pair of eyes meets another?

Daniel Goleman's masterful volume *Social Intelligence: The New Science of Human Relationships* is the definitive popular work on the emerging field of social neuroscience. While the book does not deal extensively with eye contact in and of itself, almost everything in the book is relevant to an understanding of the power of eye contact in our lives.

In the past, the field of neuroscience looked primarily at what occurred within *one brain* at a time. Recent science, however, has shown that a great deal of our brain anatomy and activity can be understood fully only by looking at what happens when the brain relates to one or more *other* brains, i.e., when we socialize.

According to Goleman, social intelligence is not just about *knowing* what works in different kinds of social situations ("savvy"), nor is it just about *doing* the most effective thing. Of course, it encompasses both those aptitudes, but if these were our only criteria, then we would have to lump the visionary leader, the loving mother, and the doctor with impeccable bedside manner along with the "callow aptitudes of the con man"[14] and the manipulative huckster. What the community leader, the mother, and the doctor do that the con man and the huckster don't do, Goleman says, is foster mutually supportive social connections and relationships, which flourish for the long haul.

Goleman lists several distinct components of social intelligence. In three of these—"primal empathy," "attunement," and "synchrony"—the emotional information transmitted through the eyes, and the connection made when two pairs of eyes behold each other, are highly relevant. A few words on each of these components illuminate these topics for us.

Primal Empathy

Think of one of your closest relations—perhaps your child, a sibling, a parent, your spouse or significant other, or a very close friend. Do you ever look at this person and just "sense" what he or she is feeling, without him or her telling you? Goleman calls this "primal empathy." It is closely related to Gladwell's "mind reading."

Living with Jena, I have come to sense the finest gradations in her interior world—from her facial expressions, her posture, her tone of voice, her eyes. Anyone with the slightest degree of sensitivity who interacts frequently with someone he or she cares about develops a similar capacity.

In *The Object Stares Back: On the Nature of Seeing*, art historian James Elkins writes about this dynamic beautifully:

> *I can understand many things my wife thinks before she even says a word, and can guess at her mood from changes so slight that I imagine no one else could see them. . . . I can sometimes tell her she's anxious or tired before she has even realized it herself. "You look sad," I'll say, and she'll say something like, "Am I? Oh yes, I suppose I am." It's a beautiful kind of knowledge, since it brings us closer to each other, and as the years go by, her face says more and more to me. When I first met her, it was almost a mask, and I saw only its main lines. Now it almost never stops speaking to me, even when she is asleep. . . .*
>
> *If I am looking at my wife and not saying a word . . . I am sending very gentle motions, faint undulations in the pool, and each one comes back to me as quickly as I send it. The two of us are like the two sides of a bowl, and the water between shimmers with an intricate pattern of crossing waves. Some of the most important moments of my life have been spent looking into her face as she looks back into mine and watching the liquid motions of her eyes as they make their silent points. In comparison to that kind of communication, everything else is crass.[15]*

This is primal empathy in its highest form. According to Goleman, this capacity is much more visceral than an intellectual understanding of the other person's emotions; it involves actually *feeling*, inside of us, some version of what the other person feels. One of the greatest discoveries in the field of social neuroscience, and one that Goleman spends a great deal of time discussing in his book, is the identification of "mirror neurons." These are neurons interspersed throughout various systems in our brain that are highly sensitive to—and take as their primary input—*the emotional states of other people*. And their primary output is *recreating those same emotional states within ourselves*.

Have you ever been going about your business, in a neutral mood, and come into contact with someone in a totally foul mood? Perhaps it was an irate customer before you in line, or perhaps the checkout person at the front of the line gave you a nasty grimace. How did you feel afterwards?

Or consider the opposite: you are in a neutral mood, and you encounter someone totally upbeat and positive—perhaps someone beaming a huge smile when she says "hello" to you. How do you feel then?

One way we are able to intuit the emotional states of others is that our mirror neurons actually recreate others' states within ourselves. Yet, how do these mirror neurons *know* what others are feeling? What are they picking up on that tells them whether someone else is happy, angry, sad, or fearful?

It appears that a great deal of this information is gleaned from the body language—particularly the facial expressions—of others. "Mirror neurons ensure that the moment someone sees an expression on your face, they will at once sense that same feeling within themselves," Goleman writes.[16] The relevance of the eyes to this process is obvious. If the face is the most emotionally expressive part of the body, then the eye area is the most emotionally expressive part of the face. A significant portion of the social circuitry of the brain is given over to detecting the emotions of others via their eyes.

Attunement

Is there someone in your life who always leaves you feeling *good* after you talk with him or her? Perhaps a loved one, a close friend, or a trusted advisor or counselor. When you talk to this person, you feel heard and understood, as though this person really *gets* you. This is what Goleman refers to as "attunement," another crucial part of our social intelligence. He calls this an "agendaless presence"—it's an ability to just *be with* another person, experiencing him or her, listening to what he or she is saying, without trying to impose an outcome or desired goal on the interaction.[17] It's the power of attention we've discussed earlier in this chapter.

In my experience, eye contact is a key component of attunement. Have you ever been at a party, talking with someone, while that person begins scanning the room, looking for other people? How does that make you feel? In moments like these, do you feel this person is deeply listening to you, getting what you're saying?

This skill is not just relevant to love, friendship, and psychotherapy suites. It's highly relevant in even the most hard-nosed areas of business. Goleman points out that "agendaless presence can be seen, surprisingly, in many top-performing sales people and client managers. Stars in these fields do not approach a customer or client with the determination to make a sale; rather, they see themselves as consultants of sorts, whose task is first to listen and understand the client's needs—and only then match what they have to those needs."[18]

Synchrony

We saw that primal empathy is a key component in social intelligence. Instantly grasping and internalizing what someone else is feeling is crucial for anticipating that person's needs and responding appropriately; if someone feels that you "get them," no matter how close or distant the relation, that person is bound to feel more connected and trusting of you.

However, there is another reason that primal empathy is powerful in social interaction. Just as the other person's emotional state serves as the input for our own mirror neurons, our own emotional states also form the input for *other people's* mirror neurons. This can create a system of feedback between two people, in which two or more individuals' internal states get in synch, mutually influencing the other. Goleman calls this state "synchrony." He also calls it "looping," as in creating a *feedback loop* between one or more people. Other researchers he cites refer to it as "empathic resonance."[19]

Perhaps the most pure form of synchrony is the pleasure we derive from dancing, in which our bodies literally sway, shake, shimmy, rock, and roll in rhythm with other bodies. Dancing, in turn, serves as a great metaphor for other less obvious forms of getting our minds, bodies, and emotions in synch. A great conversation, for example, can feel like a dance: a dance of words back and forth, a dance of glances, a dance of purrs and ahhhs and mmmss and "yes, that's right!"s And, just as in a dance where two people are stepping on each other's feet and bumping into each other irregularly, a conversation in which the timing is off and the participants never reach a state of resonance with each other feels *awful*.

Have you ever thought about why you pay exorbitant ticket prices, endure grueling weekend traffic and parking hassles, and stand in long lines in order to see a movie, concert, or play in a theater? These days, DVD and CD technology can give us a nearly flawless reproduction of these art forms digitally, on home theater screens and speaker systems that seem to be approaching closer to the size and audiovisual quality of real life each year. Why don't we just buy the CD or DVD (in some cases cheaper than ticket prices) and stay at home?

The sound and visual quality is still better in a theater, of course. But I don't think that fully explains why we keep spending billions of dollars a year on in-theater movies, concerts, musicals, and plays. I think a bigger reason is what scientists call "emotional contagion." Our mirror neurons allow emotions to sweep through a crowd within moments, synching the entire crowd to the same emotion.

In high school and early college, I was a fan of the rock band Grateful Dead. Whatever you may think of the band and its music and followers, some of the most personally meaningful moments from that period in my life—moments that I will remember for the rest of my life—came from seeing them play live. When the band got on stage, a collective joy rushed through the crowd instantly, an emotional contagion. As songs reached their crescendo, it felt as though all of us in the room had morphed into one living, breathing being locked in some kind of collective, primal shout for joy.

Of course, nearly all of us have our own forums for experiencing this kind of collective emotional resonance; it's not just a phenomenon of sixties-era jam bands. Concerts of all stripes provide this, from rock to classical, as do movies and plays, sporting events, political rallies, and of course religious services. On a smaller scale, dinner parties, family meals, and even dinner, coffee, or drinks for two at a bustling restaurant, café, or bar provide an opportunity for synching our inner states with those around us.

How is all of this related to eye contact? Our mirror neurons need something to pick up in order to determine the emotional

states of others around us. In larger group settings, such as concerts and movies, our mirror neurons are probably picking up
on the posture, vocalizations, body movements, and perhaps
even breathing patterns of those around us.

But in more intimate settings, such as dinners, parties,
conversations, and day-to-day social interactions, our eyes
are a prime source of information on others' emotional states,
and thus serve a crucial role in bringing us in emotional synchrony with those around us. "Locking eyes loops us," Goleman writes. "To reduce a romantic moment to an aspect of its
neurology, when two people's eyes meet, they have interlinked
their orbitofrontal areas, which are especially sensitive to face-
to-face cues like eye contact."[20] The orbitofrontal area is a part
of the brain that processes social information, such as reading
the emotional states of others, interpreting the social behaviors
and actions of others, and coming up with instant judgments as
to whether we like someone or not, and why.

There is perhaps no faster way of linking our internal emotional states with those of another person than making direct
eye contact. It's very simple: If in business, public speaking,
family relations, or romance, you want to feel connected with
the other person in front of you, and you want that person to
feel connected to you, improve the quality of your eye contact.
We already knew this intuitively, but in the past ten years, neuroscience has been filling in the scientific picture of why this
should be so.

The Dark Side of Eye Contact:
Eye Dancing versus Eye Groping

In this chapter, we've seen how and why eye contact has such
power to bring us together in rapport. It signals attention and

presence, in a world starved for both. However, there can be a dark side to eye contact, and it is precisely this same quality of attention that can lead to this dark side. Attention, after all, can be wanted or *unwanted*.

If I had a nickel for every time someone referred to my Eye Gazing Parties as "Eye Staring Parties," well, I'd have a lot of nickels. The reality, for many of us, is that our experience of eye contact does not involve the connection, vulnerability, and mutual opening of eye contact with a willing partner. Rather, for many, our experience with eye contact involves *staring*, that is, someone looking at us (say, in the subway, or the street) when we don't want to be looked at. Unwanted attention. The feeling is *very* uncomfortable.

There's no question that for many of us, the concept of eye contact is not all rosy. There is a dark side. As David Schnarch writes in *The Passionate Marriage*, "Most people know the icky feeling of being undressed or violated by someone *looking* at them (icky if you don't want it from that person). You know when to avert your gaze when approaching an 'intruder' on the street—you can feel it."[21] Women, in particular, have often had to deal with constant, unwelcome visual attention from males, starting in middle school or even earlier.

Indeed, for hundreds of years, "the gaze" has been a recurring theme within literature and literary criticsm, often taken as the expression of a fundamental power imbalance between the gazer and the gazee. Penetrative, objectifying visual attention from males has even been dubbed the "male gaze" by academics and has been the subject of countless scholarly articles, particularly within literary criticism and critical theory.[22]

I got my own, very minor, taste of this "male gaze" one afternoon when I went clothes shopping in the Castro district, San Francisco's famous gay neighborhood, documented so beautifully in the film *Milk*. Normally, I walk down the street and enjoy anonymity and privacy. But in the Castro, all eyes were upon me; the streets were a sea of eyes: lustful eyes, hungry eyes, beckoning eyes.

I found this experience amusing and instructive more than anything else, but it was just for an afternoon. I can only imagine what it would be like to be a woman in the subway, or on the sidewalk, receiving this kind of attention *all the time*.

Straight or gay, man or woman, a stare can also connote a potentially violent threat. In his book *On Seeing: Things Seen, Unseen, and Obscene*, F. González-Crussi, professor emeritus of pathology at the Northwestern Medical School, ties this back to distant evolution.

> *The fixity of the eye upon us makes us apprehensive. It is as if a remote memory was stirring deep inside us; an atavistic remembrance of a danger sign that harks back to pre-history, when to be bracketed persistently into someone else's visual field meant that we were being watched by a predator; that some saber-toothed beast or some behemoth of a reptile was intently considering us for lunch. . . . What, if not a profound biologic mark, tells animals to beware of the staring eye?*

He further points out that

> *natural evolution contrive[d] to paint fake eyes on the body of some species, in order to deter predators. For instance, the feathers of some birds, like the wings of some butterflies. . . . display large, circular, eye-like spots, that appear to have no other purpose than to frighten away pursuers.*
>
> *To the predator's voracious gaze, the prey somehow managed to oppose a contrary, mesmerizing, or intimidating gaze, as the lovers' eyes always manage to answer, to reply, and to engage each other in a mutual, highly nuanced, yet silent conversation.*[23]

Clearly, there is no *single thing* that eye contact means. It can mean many things, depending on the context. It can mean friendliness, lust (welcome and unwelcome), love, compassion, hostility, and a host of other things. Frans de Waal summed this up nicely:

DE WAAL: As far as eye contact is concerned, there are many misconceptions. If you read up on the Internet about eye contact and primates, for example, many people will tell you that you should never make eye contact with a primate because they will get angry and perceive it as a threat, and this is not really true.

This is true in certain competitive contexts only, and not for all primates. Many monkeys like baboons and macaques have very strict hierarchies, and one way for the dominant to intimidate the subordinate is to give them a brief stare. Yes, if you imitate that stare, and you bob your head while you do it at a monkey, they will perceive it as a threat.

But there are many other primates, such as the great apes, which are more closely related to us, where eye contact is a very common way of engaging with each other, and eye contact can be extremely friendly. Bonobos, for example, have eye contact when they have sex with each other.

I'm sure I can walk in the street here and make eye contact with humans in a way that they will consider threatening. With humans, just as in other primates, eye contact can mean many things, depending on the context, how you make it, and what you do with it.

———————

While I advocate friendly, compassionate, warm eye contact in this book, I want to acknowledge here that in many contexts eye contact can also be unwelcome, off-putting, jarring, and even terrifying. We must always be sensitive to context in our eye contact.

Given all this, what exactly is the difference between un-welcome, invasive staring and the tender, loving eye contact I'm talking about and encouraging in this book?

I like to think of it as the difference between groping and dancing. Both involve physical contact between two people, perhaps even two strangers. But a grope is a *one-way touch*. There is no back and forth (unless the recipient of the grope punches the groper, as she probably wants to do). Furthermore, the intention on the part of the groper has nothing to do with giving or sharing; it's primarily about *taking* from the other person—"copping a feel."

In contrast, the kind of eye contact I write about and ad-vocate is more like a dance. "It takes two to tango," the saying goes, and it takes two to have a meaningful, satisfying experi-ence with eye contact. In order for eye contact to feel good, one person cannot impose his visual will on another; it is a shared experience. Perhaps eyes meet only for a second at first; one partner then tests the waters and tries a few seconds, and when that is met warmly, the pair can begin ramping up the eye contact together until they are locked in a beautiful dance of eyes and gazes.

In gazing that feels good to both parties, the intention is not to *take* but rather to *give:* giving our presence, our listening, our compassion, and our own vulnerability. It is about giving the other person entry into our own inner world, and receiving the invitation to enter the other's, as if stepping into a temple in a foreign land.

In partner dancing, whether with music and bodies, or dancing with the eyes, the overriding theme is mutuality. Each partner adjusts his or her actions and energy to match the other person's, so the two partners create the dance together.

So, if you have unpleasant associations of eye contact with glaring, staring, and leering, I am right there with you; not one of us enjoys these experiences. I would never suggest that you repeat those experiences. What I'm talking about in this book is something completely different, something that—like dancing—can be a source of enormous joy, connection, and bonding.

Are you ready to begin the dance?

TWO

How to Become a Master of Eye Contact in Two Weeks

So you want to improve your skill at eye contact. Perhaps you already knew intuitively that good eye contact helps you succeed in nearly every type of social interaction you could engage in—from business to family relations to dating. Or perhaps the information about rapport and social intelligence in the last chapter convinced you.

Either way, you are faced with the question: What practical steps can I take to improve my skill at eye contact?

This chapter provides the answer.

How to Stop Being "Eye Shy"

When I started throwing Eye Gazing Parties, I got one of two polarized responses from people who heard about them. They said either "Wow, that sounds amazing, I'd love to try that out," or "Are you crazy?!?! Look into a stranger's eyes for minutes on end?!?! I could never do that!"

In this chapter, I focus on the second response. The reality is that most of us—including the most confident among us—are "eye shy" to a certain degree. Some of us find the prospect of meeting eyes with a stranger downright terrifying. I know it was for me before I got into it—I was *awful* at it, and terribly scared of it. You'd be lucky if you got two seconds worth of eye contact from me in an entire conversation!

Fear, shyness, embarrassment, dread, humiliation, terror, wanting to go hide under a rock—these emotions all commonly surround the idea of eye contact.

Why are we so terrified? What is the worst thing that could happen if we were to look in a stranger in the eyes?

Well, if that stranger happens to be a menacing thug on a dangerous urban city block—the kind of person who might respond to our gaze with "Hey, you lookin' at me?"—bad things might indeed happen. But, outside of this particular situation, what are we so afraid of?

As we've seen, your eyes are a reliable indicator of how you're actually feeling inside. Sad, happy, shy, elated, nervous—if you're feeling it, your eyes will show it.

This is why we prize eye contact so much as an indicator of both trustworthiness and also confidence. When you look someone in the eye, you're giving that person the keys to your emotional world. No wonder the person trusts you more when you do that. And no wonder the other person perceives you as more confident—it takes guts to be so vulnerable with another person.

Yet this same vulnerability, I believe, is also the reason we're so scared of eye contact. What if we give someone the keys to our emotional home, and they aren't good houseguests? What if they laugh at us, or leave a mess? These are real risks of eye contact, not to be scoffed at. I don't like being rejected socially any more than anyone else. It hurts.

Other concerns about eye contact include our legitimate

desire for privacy, for self-protection, for guarding our vulnerable inner selves from the prying gaze of others. These are all legitimate motivations. They all have their place.

But do these fears really explain our intense aversion to eye contact with strangers? And is allowing these fears to take over really the best thing for our lives? Is it possible we could gain a great deal by easing our tight clutch on these fears and letting others into our inner world?

When we compare the relatively modest social risks of eye contact with the intense aversion many of us feel toward it, it makes sense to talk about this aversion as a kind of social anxiety or phobia.

Fortunately, there is a proven, well-documented method for overcoming anxieties of all sorts. That method is called "systematic desensitization."

Here's the idea: Systematically put yourself in contact with the object of anxiety, first in your imagination, and then—with baby steps—in the real world. The point is, you see that you *don't die* from doing it—and in fact, you might even enjoy it. Psychologists have had success with this method in helping people with all kinds of anxieties and phobias, from public speaking to flying on airplanes.

The psychologist Albert Ellis tells a story of how he even performed this technique on himself to get over his fear of approaching and talking with attractive women. Over the course of one month, he forced himself to walk up and start a conversation with every attractive woman he saw alone in the Brooklyn Botanic Garden. All in all, he did one hundred of these approaches, and toward the end he was approaching women with ease and starting conversations with them. (He says he didn't get a single date out of all of this—perhaps his next step should have been conversation classes!)

Becoming Eye Bold

We're going to get over our fear and discomfort around eye contact—"systematically desensitize" ourselves to it—in several manageable steps:

1. Making progressively lengthy eye contact with a friend or family member, in an intentional exercise.
2. Making infinitesimally brief eye contact with strangers on the street.
3. Making longer eye contact with strangers such as waiters, salesclerks, and cashiers.
4. Making substantial eye contact during conversations with friends, family members, co-workers, and other people you know.
5. Making substantial eye contact during conversations with people you've just met.

Step 1: Make Progressively Lengthy Eye Contact with a Friend or Family Member

We're going to start by jumping headfirst into the pool. But don't worry: It's a safe, inviting pool, with a lifeguard watching your every move. You'll be fine! This exercise is called "eye gazing." People from all over the world have tried it at my parties, with no eye contact experience at all, and not one person has gone to the hospital!

Here's how we're going to do it: Find a friend or a family member who is at least somewhat open-minded (i.e., not your cousin Bob who makes cynical and sarcastic jokes at anything even slightly out of the ordinary).

Explain to your friend that you want to improve your eye contact. Explain all the reasons to get better at eye contact—from dating to asking for a raise, or anything else that is motivating you personally. Or perhaps you don't have any specific reasons; you're just curious. Whatever it is, make sure your friend knows why he or she is being dragged into this experiment.

Once you've got your friend on board, here's what you are going to do:

1. Sit across from each other, about a foot to two feet apart, either in two chairs or on the floor. It's better if there's not a table in between you, as having anything in between you does lower the intensity of the exercise. (If you're feeling *really* uncomfortable, then having a table between you might help.) In terms of physical distance, you want to feel close and intimate, but not so close that you feel your space is being invaded.

2. First, look at each other straight in the eyes for just *one second*, and then look away. For this exercise, look at only one of your partner's eyes at a time. You can switch which eye you look at, but don't try to look at both eyes at once.

3. Now, look at each other in the eyes for *five seconds*, then look away. Laugh, giggle, make sarcastic jokes.

4. Now *ten seconds*.

5. Now *thirty seconds*.

6. Now *one minute*.

7. Now *three minutes*.

Here are some pointers on how you can do this exercise best:

- Keep a neutral facial expression. Often we associate direct eye contact with either aggression or seduction. Neither one will put your partner at ease. Don't worry about smiling or maintaining a pleasant expression. Just let your face relax and let your eyes do the talking.
- Keep a "soft gaze." You can actually control how harsh your gaze feels by how intensely you focus on one point. Have you ever heard someone say, "His eyes were bearing down on me?" It's not a pleasant feeling! So keep a softer, warmer focus, even as you look into one eye.
- Breathe! This is a nerve-wracking, intense thing you're playing with here, so there can be a tendency to hold your breath as if you were about to dive off a cliff. Relax, and be sure to take deep breaths throughout. Once you get into it, the exercise can actually feel deeply relaxing and calming, like a meditation.
- This isn't a staring contest. It's OK to blink, laugh, giggle, scratch your nose. Most people find that they giggle starting out. This is totally normal. It's a nervous, unfamiliar thing we're doing, so it's natural to let off some tension by laughing. Usually, the laughter subsides within the period of a three-minute gaze.
- Notice whatever thoughts arise while you're gazing. Perhaps you're thinking "This is totally weird!" Or perhaps you're thinking "What is my friend thinking about this?" Whatever you think is fine. Just notice the thoughts, let them pass, and bring your attention back to the gaze.
- You may notice the image of your friend's face

morphing, or other visual illusions with color or
light. No, you haven't taken LSD. This is totally
normal. I've noticed that it usually happens when
I'm really concentrated and focused on the gazing.
It means you are very much "in the zone" with the
gazing!

Now go to it!

Congratulations, you've just made *three minutes* of direct eye
contact with someone. Already, you're ahead of most of the
population in terms of your eye contact skills and experience!
I'm serious. I'll bet if you took a whole football stadium full of
random people, only five to ten of them would have had that
much prolonged eye contact at once. You're already on your
way to being a pro.

Step 2: Make Infinitesimally Brief Eye Contact with Strangers

In this step, we're going to begin the process of making eye
contact with strangers. Don't worry—it's not as scary as it
sounds. We'll only be making a fraction of a second's worth of
eye contact while passing strangers on the sidewalk—certainly
not long enough for anyone to pull out a dagger and stab
you.

Here's the exercise. While you walk down the sidewalk
(during daylight hours!) look at the eyes of every person walking toward you *long enough to see their eye color*. Then look away.
That's it.

I've been practicing this one for years, and never have I
had a negative experience from it. It's the single best technique

I know of for becoming more comfortable with eye contact quickly. You'd be amazed at how willing people on the street are to connect with you briefly through the eyes.

All the pointers raised in the eye contact exercise above are still valid and important, *particularly* the ones about neutral facial expression and soft gaze. You don't want people to think you're trying to stare them down, rob them, or get them into the sack. (OK, maybe that last one in some cases . . . but let's save that one for later!) Just keep a neutral, plain-Jane facial expression as you do this exercise, and you'll be amazed at the results.

Here are some more pointers to keep in mind:

- Don't initiate eye contact too far away. Otherwise, you'll make the other person feel like you're staring at him or her. Initiate the eye contact when you're four to five paces away. It should last only one pace at most.
- Break your eye contact laterally, not vertically. What this means is, if you make eye contact with someone walking by you on your left side, break your eye contact by looking straight ahead, *not* by looking down.

Why? Typically the lower-status individual in any interaction breaks eye contact first by looking down; this is as true in humans as in other primates. This is the classic "look of shame." It communicates "You win; you're better than me; you have more power than me."

Now, the point of this particular exercise is not to establish dominance over strangers. In fact, to be polite, *you* should break the eye contact first, so you're not making a bunch of random people feel as though you're staring them down. But, if you continuously practice breaking the eye contact verti-cally (i.e., by looking down), you'll be continuously practicing a body tic associated with shame and submission. Not recom-mended!

Try breaking a few instances of eye contact by looking down, just to see what it feels like. Then try it by looking away horizontally. You will probably feel a huge difference inside.

Most likely you will get one of three reactions to your eye contact in the sidewalk. In most cases, the other person will meet your eye contact with a neutral expression and look away. In some cases, the other person may meet your eye con-tact with a smile and look away. And in some cases, the other person may maintain eye contact with you. (For you slowpokes out there, this last one means the other person is attracted to you!) In the first case, just break eye contact as normal. In the second case, you may want to return the smile. And if you're lucky enough to experience the third case, well, why not stop and say hello?

I've had wonderful experiences using this technique. What most strikes me about it is how it transforms the urban land-scape. Before I started doing this, I would walk around the city and mostly view the other people I encountered as obstacles or annoyances. But once I started doing it—once I started looking into the windows of hundreds of people's souls each day—the whole scene shifted. I suddenly saw so much beauty out there, so much sadness. So many heavy burdens, so much joy, so many hopes and dashed hopes, dreams, and desires—so much decency. The city became a symphony of emotion—all from this one simple shift.

And yes, this habit of mine has lead to dates. More on this topic in Chapter 4!

Step 3: Make Longer Eye Contact with Strangers, Such as Waiters, Salesclerks, and Cashiers

There's absolutely nothing wrong with "practicing" eye contact with waiters, salesclerks, cashiers, and other paid service people, so long as you do it respectfully and in a friendly way. Hey, I've worked as a waiter, and I wished more of my customers had made eye contact with me. If you do it with the right intentions—to establish a real human connection with someone you're interacting with—it will brighten that person's life in what is otherwise probably a challenging or dull workday.

So, next time a waiter or checkout person asks you "How are you doing today?" look the person right in the eyes and give an honest answer. "I'm doing great!" or "Oh, not so good today." Whatever the honest answer is, give it with a warm look right from your eyes.

Sometimes, the other person will look right away. Don't be ashamed or feel bad. You haven't done anything wrong. You made an honest, well-intended overture at making a human connection, and it was turned down, that's all. (One aspect of learning about eye contact is learning to deal with rejection comfortably.) Waiters and other service staff come into contact with hundreds of strangers a day, and if they had to make a genuine connection with all of them, they'd be completely exhausted, go crazy, or both! So many of them understandably "tune out" any authentic interaction with their customers. I certainly did on some days when I was working as a waiter.

But you'll be surprised. Many waiters and other service people are also sick of the hundreds of inauthentic, insincere, and impersonal interactions they have with customers each day. I know I was. They are starved for authentic, meaningful human contact on their job. When I've practiced this with waiters and other service people, I've been amazed at how many brighten up and beam smiles back, just because someone is treating them as a fellow human being rather than as a service robot.

I've also noticed that some people working in retail sales are *extremely* comfortable with prolonged eye contact, and will meet yours for as long as you can stand.

If you legitimately want to do business at their establishment, consider this an eye-contact blessing. I've often maintained eye contact off and on for three or four minutes with salespeople like this while discussing the merits of various products I'm shopping for. I've gained huge experience and comfort with eye contact using this technique.

Step 4: Make Substantial Eye Contact During Conversations with Friends, Family Members, Co-workers, and Other People You Know

You're pretty much an eye contact expert now. You've made prolonged eye contact in an intense exercise, you've connected briefly with strangers on the street, and you've even had long eye contact with strangers such as waiters and salesclerks.

Now it's time to amp it up a notch.

In this segment, we're going to talk about how to increase the eye contact next time you're talking with a friend, family member, or co-worker.

This must be done slowly and gradually, as the person you're talking with may be accustomed to years' worth of little eye contact, and it will be awkward if you go from zero to sixty in no time.

Eye contact in casual conversations with friends and family members is a delicate dance. It's reciprocal, and you want to entice the other person into eye dancing with you. Too much right off the bat and you'll scare the other person away (and probably field questions about what the heck has gotten into you.)

To ease into this eye dance, we're first going to learn about a concept called "psychological space," which is highly relevant.

The concept was pioneered by legendary anthropologist Edward T. Hall, founder of the field of proxemics, which studies the distances between animals (including human animals) as they interact.[1]

The basic idea of psychological space is this: Many factors aside from raw physical distance influence our subjective perception of distance from another person. Lance Mason, a dating coach we'll meet in more depth in Chapter 4, told me that five of the most important factors are these:

- whether the other person is facing us
- whether our attention is on the other person
- whether the other person is talking about something relevant to us
- whether the other person is making physical contact with us
- whether the other person is making eye contact with us

Here's a fun exercise to learn about how these five different factors of psychological space feel, and how they influence our perceived proximity to others. I did this once at a workshop designed by Mason. Learning about psychological space will immeasurably improve the comfort and ease of your body language.

Exercise: Psychological Space

Recruit a friend. Tell him or her you've got an exercise that will teach you both a lot about body language. You're going to try five different interactions that demonstrate the five psychological space factors above.

1. Stand facing each other, about three feet apart. Now turn away in place and stand facing apart. Notice how this one shift radically changes your feeling of distance from the other person, even though you stayed the same distance apart. (If you ever really want to play with this one, try standing facing the back in a crowded elevator. You could cut the discomfort and awkwardness with a butter knife.)

2. Turn to face each other again, still about three feet apart. Now move close to each other, and as you get near each other, turn to face the same side of the room. Now both of you point at and comment on the same object across the room. ("Hey, look at that TV set.") Notice how you actually felt closer while facing each other three feet apart than you do shoulder-to-shoulder while looking across the room!

3. Stand back to back, with about six inches in between you. Ask your friend to ramble about some story completely irrelevant to your life. Notice how far away or close this person seems to you. Now ask him or her to mock-insult you by, say, making fun of what you're wearing. All of a sudden, your ears prick up and this person will feel a lot closer physically!

4. Stand side by side, with about six inches in between you. Notice how close or distant you feel. Now, have your friend touch your back or arm. Notice how that makes you feel

a lot closer, even though your physical distance has not changed.

5. Stand three feet apart, facing. Alternate between talking to each other with no eye contact, and talking with each other while making eye contact. Notice how this radically shifts your sense of psychological space.

6. Finally, play with all these elements at once. Try the most extreme: standing close to each other, looking right at each other, while touching each other's arms or shoulders, and mock-insulting each other. You will feel like you're practically in the same body! Then, progressively peel one of these proximity factors off while keeping the others intact: First, stop touching. Then, stop talking about each other and switch to a neutral topic. Then, cut the eye contact. Then, turn away from each other partially, so that you're both facing the same side of the room. Then, step a few paces away from each other. Notice how each of these moves changes the perception of distance.

It should be obvious how all of this relates to the topic of this book. Eye contact is one of the most powerful influences on psychological space!

Armed with this knowledge, you are ready to start increasing your eye contact with friends, family members, and co-workers in your day-to-day conversations. The key is that if you start increasing eye contact, and you don't want the other person to feel trapped or uncomfortable, you'll need to balance that out by moderating other factors influencing social space, such as physical distance.

Here are some pointers on how to do it:

• Lean back a little. As you increase the eye contact, decrease the physical proximity a little by leaning back. This will give the other person room to breathe.

- Don't bear down on the other person with your eyes, or make him or her constantly submit and look away. Eye contact is a dance. Invite the other person into this dance with a brief moment of eye contact, then look away. Then back to eye contact for a little longer, then look away. It's completely normal and comfortable to make and break eye contact back and forth within a conversation—don't view this as a sign of failure. Over the course of the conversation, increase the length of each moment of eye contact before breaking away, in a mutual easing in of comfort and trust, not a forced bearing-down.
- Smile! Breathe! Feel the deeper connection develop.

———

Step 5: Make Substantial Eye Contact During Conversations with People You've Just Met

This final step is simple. Just take the skills you've developed in the last step, and port them over to talking with people who are new in your life—new acquaintances and connections at cocktail parties, conferences, business events, birthday parties, dinner parties, and every other kind of event. Remember all the pointers about psychological space, and inviting your partner into an eye dance with give and take, not a one-way staring contest.

Congratulations! You've completed all five steps, and you are now an Eye Contact Master.

You will be amazed at the feeling of connection, sharing, and trust you are quickly able to develop with loved ones and strangers alike through sharing eye contact. I've never encountered a faster route to trust, openness, communication, and vulnerability, and it is my great pleasure to have shared with you a clear road map to these benefits in this chapter.

Questions and Answers

Should I look at just one eye, or try to look at both?

Without a doubt, this is the most common question I receive about "how to do it"—the practical side of eye contact. For that reason, I've spent a lot of time thinking about, talking with others about, and field-testing different answers to this question.

Here's the conclusion I've come to after all of this effort: In virtually all initial, casual situations, such as an initial business meeting or the beginning of a conversation with a new person at a party, it is better to look at both your conversation partner's eyes at once.

Now, it is not possible to actually *focus* on two different points at once. If you try, you'll go cross-eyed. Here is the secret: When talking with someone new, maintain a relatively soft, gentle, wide focus in general, taking in your conversation partner's entire face, with the eyes in the center of your field of vision.

I have found—and everyone who has tested this with me agrees—that this is more comfortable for casual conversational eye contact. Focusing on just one eye during a casual conversation can feel as though you are boring into someone with your gaze.

So how do you do this?

Here's an exercise:

1. Hold a normal-sized book in front of you at arms' length.

2. Focus your eyes on one letter of the title. This is roughly what focusing your eyes on just one eye feels like. It is an intense feeling—all of your attention is drilling in to one small spot, with little of your awareness or attention available to the rest of your visual field.

3. Now, widen your field of vision to include the entire book. Most likely, you will need to "soften" your focus in order to really see the whole book at once. You probably won't be able to make out all of the features of the book in detail, but you are taking in the entire book cover with your awareness. Feel what this feels like. It's a "softer" feeling—you are not drilling through anything with your laser vision.

Now that you've got a feeling for this, you can practice with a friend:

1. Recruit a friend to practice with you.

2. Begin a casual conversation about how your day has been so far.

3. As you are talking, try going between focusing on one of your partner's eyes, and widening your field of vision to include your partner's entire face, with the eyes at the center of the field of vision.

A word of caution: many articles about body language I've seen on the Internet suggest looking at the bridge of your partner's nose as a way to create the effect that you're looking at both eyes at the same time. It's true: This does create that illusion. But it is an illusion! You are looking at the bridge of your partner's nose, not the eyes. People who use this technique are really practicing nose contact, not eye contact!

To connect with both of your partner's eyes at once, try what I've discussed here instead: take in your partner's entire face, with your partner's eyes at the center of your field of vision.

As we've seen, this involves a "softer" focus, meaning you do not bring the face into as crisp detailed focus. What you sacrifice in visual detail, however, you gain in feelings of comfort and connection with each other, as a highly focused gaze is typically too intense and perhaps even too intimate for normal social and business conversation.

Once you are in a very deep or engaged conversation with someone, where trust and rapport has developed, then that same intensity and intimacy is actually a good thing. So when you start to feel really connected with someone and find yourself in an involved conversation—this may not be on the first or even fifth conversation—you can switch to looking at just one of your partner's eyes at a time.

If I choose to gaze at one of my partner's eyes at a time, do I stay with just one or do I go back and forth?

If you're in an intimate or intense conversation with someone and want to gaze in just one eye at a time, doing so without change feels weird for both you and the recipient of such a gaze. Also, looking at one point fixedly is likely to lead you to "zone out" and lose track of what the other person is saying. It will encourage you to develop the "laser vision" of intense focus we discussed before. As always, keep a soft focus, even as you focus only on one eye, and move back and forth between eyes. This, however, raises the question: how quickly? Well, you don't want your partner to feel that your eyes are following a ping-pong match. I'd say every three or four seconds feels about right. But test it out yourself and see what feels best to you.

You talk a lot about maintaining a "soft gaze." What does that mean, exactly?

To get a better sense of what this feels like, try this little experiment. Take some relatively pleasant object around your house—say, a bowl of fruit, a painting, or a vase with flowers. Sit about ten feet away from it.

First, imagine drilling through this object with superhero laser-beam eyes. You are Superman with his famous "heat vision," and the beams out of your eye are piercing right through the object. Experience what it feels like.

Now, drop the laser vision, and instead, embrace this object with your gaze. I know this may sound terribly hokey, but humor me on this one and give it a try. Imagine your gaze is sending out waves of love and acceptance, enveloping the object in tender embrace. How does that feel (besides hokey?).

You'll probably notice that the first iteration, the laser vision, feels tense. The facial muscles around your eye tense up (similar to the effects of squinting to focus). The corners of your mouth drop, and your cheeks form a small scowl.

In contrast, the second iteration, which I call an "embracing" gaze, probably feels better. The facial muscles around your eyes relax, and you might notice the corners of your mouth moving upward in a soft smile.

Now, you probably don't want to be thinking all of those warm, well-wishing, embracing thoughts every time you talk to someone—the postman, the tollbooth operator, the waiter. (Though if you do, you might find yourself feeling more positive throughout the day.) And it's not necessary. But try it once or twice a day, and that should be enough to create within you the muscle memory of what a soft, embracing gaze feels like.

If you practice the soft gaze regularly, you will be amazed at the results. Social interactions run more smoothly; people want to be around you; you will find yourself getting invited to more parties and other social events. Why? Because being on the receiving end of this gaze feels *great* (just as being on the receiving end of laser vision feels terrible). People like to be around people who make them feel great. While you don't need to do all the internal well-wishing that I wrote about above, I recommend you at least use the physical aspects of the embracing gaze—soft focus, relaxed facial muscles, soft smile—in every social interaction throughout your day. Few things will increase your sociability more than learning to make eye contact in this manner.

A piercing gaze under any circumstances—except when you are trying to project hostility and dominance (see Chapter 7)—is a big no-no.

I often look away while I'm talking during a conversation. Is that bad from your perspective?

Of course not! You will probably notice that, in a conversation, it feels very natural to look away when you are thinking about a point, or gathering your train of thought as you talk. There's a very simple reason for this. As Mihaly Csikszentmihalyi writes in his famous book *Flow: The Psychology of Optimal Experience*:

> [T]he nervous system has definite limits on how much information it can process at any given time. There are just so many "events" that can appear in consciousness and be recognized and handled appropriately before they begin to crowd each other out. . . . Thoughts have to follow each other, or they get jumbled. . . . We cannot run, sing, and balance the checkbook at the same time, because each one of these activities exhausts most of our capacity for attention.[2]

Taking in someone's eyes is one of the most psychologically salient experiences we can have—there are so many shades of nuance and meaning to interpret. It's like a big flashing movie of emotion, right in front of our face. So it's understandable

that when we are using a lot of our "processing power" to remember something, come up with our next train of thought,
or formulate our opinion on something, we have to tune out
this rich additional source of input. There's not a lot left over
for taking in and processing the complex and signal-rich information we get from someone's eyes. It is natural to look away
in these circumstances—saving our processing power for the
mental tasks at hand.

The last thing I want is for this book's message of "more
eye contact" to make you feel self-conscious, as if you're doing
something "wrong" when you look away in a conversation.
Not only is it not wrong, it's actually what you *should* be doing!
You'd come across as a complete freak if you made pure 100%
eye contact in any conversation. What I'm talking about in this
book is adding 20 to 30 percent more eye contact into your
conversations.

Eye contact is a rich spice of social life. Like any other spice,
a little extra goes a long way.

Finally, one word of caution. This was offered to me by
Marie Forleo, an author whom we'll meet in more depth in the
next chapter. I think she's spot on.

FORLEO: Many people who get into eye contact start
trying to "do" eye contact, like it's this technique that's *sooo
profound* [mock California surfer voice—giggling] and that's
going to *get* you some "deep" experience if you do it right.
This is particularly common among "New Age" types who go
to a lot of self-development workshops.

You shouldn't be trying to "do" eye contact all the time.
It's annoying to others. Let it happen naturally. Just look at the
people around you as the human beings that they are, and the
eye contact will come naturally and perfectly.

THREE

Eye Flirting, Part I

For Women Only

> Such a pair of bright eyes as hers learn their
> power very soon, and use it very early . . .
> [A] pair of bright eyes with a dozen glances suffice
> to subdue a man; to enslave him, and inflame him;
> to make him even forget; they dazzle him so that
> the past becomes straightway dim to him; and he
> so prizes them that he would give all his life to
> possess 'em. What is the fond love of dearest
> friends compared to this treasure?
> —WILLIAM MAKEPEACE THACKERAY[1]

One night, a woman named Jess McCann was out with a bunch of her girlfriends at glamorous, high-fashion parties surrounding the Sundance Film Festival. The ladies were engaged in a little contest—who could flirt with and attract the most cute guys each night.

One woman from the group, Leah, was far outpacing her peers.

McCANN: Guys were flocking to her. One after another was coming up to her, flirting with her, joking with her, and asking for her number. And they were completely ignoring the rest of us, like we were chopped liver. Yet, we all knew we were just as pretty as Leah. We couldn't figure out what was going on.

Then I got it. Leah was doing something I already did successfully in sales, which I call the SEE factor.

———

Jess was a successful sales professional, selling complex medical devices to hospitals. She later parlayed this sales success into dating success, and wrote a book called *You Lost Him At Hello: A Saleswoman's Secrets to Closing the Deal with Any Guy You Want.*

SEE stands for "Smile, Eye [Contact], and Energy." Jess writes in her book, "When you see a guy you think you might be interested in, walk by him, smile, look him right in the eye, and let him sense your good energy."[2]

ELLSBERG: I often recommend to my own single female friends that they make eye contact with guys they're interested in first, but my friends always object: "But he'll think I'm 'easy!'"

McCANN: Yes, lot of my clients tell me, "But if I look at him, he's going to think I like him." I turn right around and ask them, "Why is that bad?"

I remind my clients, "When you make eye contact with a guy, you're not telling him you're in love with him, or that you want to marry him and have kids with him, or even that you want to sleep with him. You're letting him know, in a very classy way, that you're intrigued by him and would like to know more. That you're open to him coming over and talking to you. That's all."

ELLSBERG: A lot of women I've talked with want a guy who is so confident, he'll come over and talk whether she's invited him or not. In fact, some single women even seem to put out "unavailable" body signals intentionally (closed body language, looking away, and so forth) as a kind of filter to weed out the least confident guys. They make themselves "hard to get," so that only the most confident guys approach them and get through to them.

McCANN: I would ask those women, "How's that working for you? If it was working so well, you wouldn't still be alone, would you?" The reality is, there are a lot of great guys out there, guys who would make amazing boyfriends or husbands, who just need a tiny bit of encouragement to make a move. Not a lot—just enough to know they're not going to get rejected right away when they come up to you.

Men have a very hard time coming over to women they're interested in. It's extremely intimidating. They're putting a lot of their ego on the line by coming over to you, and they risk rejection every time. By giving the guys you're interested in just that little signal that you're open to him coming over, you'll be shocked at how many great guys come up and approach you. From there, you can let them take over and do the work. But you've given them that extra push to get them going.

If I can get a client to just try this—and often, it's a tough sell—they come back to me and say they were shocked at the results, that they can't believe such a little thing could yield such an amazing difference. I get e-mails every day from women saying, "I just tried the eye contact you recommended, and cute guys were approaching me like never before." It's the easiest thing to do, yet it gets immediate, noticeable results.

ELLSBERG: Do you have any recent examples of this kind of eye contact in action?

McCANN: Just the other night, I was out in a bar with a single friend, Amanda. She spotted a guy she was interested in, at the other end of the bar. Like most women, instead of turning toward the guy, as I recommend, she turned away, trying at all costs to avoid him getting any inkling that she was interested in him. And, not surprisingly, he ignored her and just kept chatting with his friends. "What should I do?" Amanda asked me.

I told her to look at him in the eyes, smile, and exude fantastic energy for just a moment, then turn back to me. Well, she did it. The guy, who was very cute, stood straight up in his chair, like he had just been hit by a bolt of electricity, and smiled Amanda's way. A few moments later, he got out of his chair, walked about twenty feet down the length of the bar, sat right down next to Amanda, and asked her, 'Hey, how's it going tonight?' They got into a long, fascinating conversation, and he eventually asked for her number. That never would have happened had she kept pretending not to be interested in him. Amanda was sold on eye contact as a tool for flirtation.

Jess McCann's teachings on eye contact are actually part of her larger philosophy of dating, which encourages women to be more proactive in their dating instead of waiting around for Mr. Right to magically appear. She writes in her book: "If you see someone you want to meet, you must do something about it. Can you imagine if, as a salesperson, I had the attitude that I wasn't going to approach customers first, that they had to come to me? I'd be out of a job pretty fast. Most women do not want to make the first move. . . . The truth it, it's totally fine to approach a man . . . if you know how to do it."[3]

McCann has dated some very desirable men, including, she

says on her website (www.jessmccann.com), "professional athletes, TV and radio personalities, as well as one of the *Forbes* 40
richest men under 40."

McCANN: Every man I've ever dated, I approached first. I
never wait around when I see a guy I like.

ELLSBERG: This is so different from the way most women
date. How do you do this without realizing many women's fear
of seeming desperate or on the hunt?

McANN: It's simple. I use eye contact. Usually that's plenty.
But sometimes I'll add an extra step I call an "Icebreaker." This
is just a simple question, such as "Hey, do you know what time
it is?" or "Hey, what are the best drink specials here?" Something very innocuous. I'm not going up to him and telling him
I want to marry him. Usually, this is *more* than enough to get
the guy asking me questions and engaged in the conversation.
Then he takes it from there.

ELLSBERG: Where do you do this? Bars? Clubs? Parties?

McCANN: Everywhere! Anywhere I see a guy I'm interested in dating. A lot of women don't think of meeting men
outside of a social setting. They get all dressed up on a Friday or
Saturday night, and that's their time to meet guys. Well, if you
only do that, you're missing 99 percent of your opportunities
to meet guys. I encourage my clients to put a little extra effort
into looking nice, and to be ready to use eye contact *whenever*
they go out—to the grocery store, on their way to work, on
their lunch break, at the gym.

Once they get into it, they get addicted to it. These are
women who may never have had guys approaching them, and
now, just with a little bit of eye contact and a smile, they have
guys approaching them all day long. More guys than they know
what to do with. I've actually had clients who got so into it,
they'll be on a date, and without realizing it, they'll be using

eye contact with other guys in the cafe or restaurant. I never thought I'd get to the point where I actually have to tell clients, "Don't use eye contact with other men when you're on a date. Just look at the guy you're on a date with!"

The Most Magnetic Woman in the Room

Whether your eyes are facing the door or the back of the room, you will know when Annie Lalla walks in the room.

We all have friends who "light up a room" when they enter. Annie Lalla is the person I know who most has this ability. She is an attractive woman of Indian descent, by way of Trinidad and Toronto, now living in New York, but attractiveness alone does not explain it.

New York is full of beautiful women. I remember being invited to a young society fundraiser once at a chic ballroom in Manhattan. The room was packed with models and social-ites, the highest concentration of feminine physical beauty I have ever seen assembled in one place. I remember one row of simply *stunning* women, all of whom could have been on a magazine cover.

Yet, they were all sitting there detached—checking their text messages, with that "This party is *so* beneath me" look that many attractive women seem adopt reflexively in social set-tings. Collectively, they exuded as much charm and personality as the fiber health shake I drink in the mornings.

Annie Lalla, in turn, walks in a room, and all at once, it's as though everyone has just been intravenously infused with a few extra glasses of champagne combined with a few Red Bulls.

She smiles, she laughs, she makes her rounds of the room, she consciously meets new people. When she talks to you, you feel like she's *really listening*, like you're the most fascinating person in the room, like she truly cares about you. It feels wonderful.

One thing I've noticed about Annie, who runs a web magazine called Wonder (www.wonderzine.net, "for the emotionally astute female intellectual") is that she's constantly making eye contact, walking up and starting conversations with *everyone*, whether you're young or old, male or female, gorgeous or plain.

Naturally, this openness to the world—a big sign over her head saying, "Yes! Talk to me!"—leads to a lot of attention from men. She has no shortage of high-status men gaga over her, and she goes on a date any night of the week she wants: one night with an accomplished scientist, the next with a business tycoon, the next with a well-known artist.

What's interesting about Annie is how unusual her stance of openness to the world is, particularly for an attractive woman. Very few women, no matter what they look like, walk up to men and start conversations. Very few women make direct eye contact with a variety of men in a day. Most women, I've noticed, adopt a generally defensive body language toward males in their surroundings: "Don't look at me, don't talk to me, and definitely don't consider asking me out on a date!"

This is certainly understandable, given what disrespectful louts, oafs, and boors many men are when talking to women (sorry, guys—it's true! We've got to step it up. Read the next chapter to learn how!). So, to protect themselves from the many jerks who so unfortunately populate my gender, many women understandably put a "stay-away" shield around them with their facial expressions, eyes, and body language. The popularity among some stylish women of wearing sunglasses and iPod headphones adds to this wall of unapproachability.

The trouble with this stance toward the outside world is that it "throws out the baby with the bathwater." In order to wall themselves off from so much *unwanted* attention, many women wall themselves off from *wanted* attention as well. The result is an epidemic of single women wondering why "there aren't any good men out there," when in fact they've put up every single barrier, wall, and STOP sign imaginable that would keep a good man from approaching them.

Annie Lalla engages in a different, and I think more inspired and inspiring, way of relating to the outside world. Her outer social boundaries—her eyes, her body language, her facial expressions—are wide open to the world. Not only does she allow and even encourage others to approach her, she bravely initiates connections with men and women she wants to talk with.

Does this mean that Annie constantly ends up in conversations she doesn't want to be in? Does she accept dates she'd rather not go on? Of course not. While she has very open *outer* social boundaries, her *inner* boundaries are rock solid. Rather than keeping a social wall outside of her, her boundaries live closer on the inside. But they're still there, and if she decides she doesn't want to talk or have further interaction with a person, she has no problem exiting the situation, no harm done. The key is, she has the ability and confidence to navigate the conversation after the initial eye contact, and to end it gracefully yet decisively if and when she wants to.

This stance has wide implications for Annie's social life, far beyond dating. She has one of the richest, varied, and most interesting social lives of anyone I know. With more friends than she knows what to do with, she gets invited to countless parties and social events. Though she is single, she enjoys a fun dating life that nearly any single woman would envy.

Ladies, wouldn't you like some of these same results in *your* life?

ELLSBERG: Annie, tell me, how do you do all of this?

LALLA: The root of all women's bitchiness toward men in a social setting is actually shyness. Most women just don't have the savvy to extricate themselves somewhere down the line, were they to open a conversation with a man. If you don't know how to get out of a conversation, you'll be afraid of getting into one.

As soon as you smile at someone, or look into their eyes, you are saying "yes" to an interaction. You're NOT saying "yes" to sex. But unless you know how to maneuver between all the different possible outcomes of the conversation, all you're worried about is avoiding the sex one. If you don't have the skills, your body language will say "no" to everything up front.

ELLSBERG: So, let's say you say "yes" to an interaction— with your eyes, or your smile, or by starting a conversation. How do you get out of the interaction if you no longer want to talk to the guy? For example, if he starts saying, "Hey, let's go out this weekend," and you have no interest.

LALLA: I don't even let it get that far. If you were to look at an interaction between two people, and put it under a microscope, there are many levels we're using to communicate with each other long before it gets to that: how you allow them to touch your hand, how close you're standing, how long you keep eye contact. Only 10 percent of the time does a guy go past where I think is appropriate, causing me to extricate myself. I rarely have to say anything direct or rude. It's all through subtle verbal cues and body language.

If your intention in the interaction is to say, with your body language, "It's wonderful to be talking with you, but I'm *unavailable* sexually," they will pick up on that. If instead, you stand in an energy of "I'm afraid, how do I get out of him wanting to have sex with me?" you will communicate a nervous—even bitchy—energy that leaves the man confused.

ELLSBERG: And what do you do when they don't pick up on that?

LALLA: But it happens so infrequently!

ELLSBERG: OK, let's role play. I want to see this. I'll play the guy who is not picking up on the cues. Let's say we've been talking for fifteen minutes. And I say, "Hey, there's this party I'm going to on Saturday night, I'd love to take you as my date. Can I get your number and take you out?"

LALLA: "Why don't I give you my e-mail. I'm sure we can develop our connection online first." That's one of the first things I do. I go into e-mail; it's safer and allows you to explore their character further before agreeing to a date. You can deduce so much from the content of an e-mail—intelligence, wit, imagination, style.

ELLSBERG: But what if you don't even want to see or speak to the guy again?

LALLA: I would never have spent the last fifteen minutes talking to him. Within a minute I've decided whether I find him interesting or not. Remember, a guy who's just focused on picking me up is not going to offer much in the conversation, because he has an agenda. When you're focused on an agenda, you don't unfurl organically or naturally in a conversation.

I can smell the difference between a pickup convo and a "Hello human, who are you?" convo. To get fifteen minutes into a conversation with me, you have to be coming from the latter. The pure pickup approach, I would have ducked out of that already. "I need to go get my drink," or something.

ELLSBERG: It sounds like you're really comfortable ending the conversation after even a minute, if there's nothing there for you.

LALLA: Oh yes, but I'm always compassionate. I'll grab their hand and say, "I so loved talking to you, but I've gotta run, must go help the hostess in the kitchen." I'll find some soft yummy excuse, but still hold their hand or give them a little hug.

I never want them to feel hurt or discouraged. I want to

leave their esteem intact, so they continue approaching women. When I leave a guy, the rejection should feel like the most loving rejection possible.

It takes a lot for a man to walk up to a woman and start a connection, and that needs to be acknowledged and appreciated. It's like a gold star for trying, because their fear usually wins. Even if I'm not going to go home and sleep with him, even if I'm not going to be his girlfriend, I'm saying "yay" for overcoming the fear and trying to connect. You see, if you're actually "yaying" for them when you extricate yourself from the conversation, they're going to hear the "yay." I just want them to hear the "yay" more than the "nay."

ELLSBERG: Many women are afraid of making the guy feel bad, so they keep talking with him even when they don't want to. Because of this, they're afraid of initiating the interaction to begin with, with their eyes or a smile.

LALLA: Right. The difference is, they're going into the interaction worried about having to extricate themselves. They're worried about avoidance, not how the conversation could unfurl. I know, down the line, no matter what happens—unless they *abduct* me into an alley—I'll be able to extricate myself. I have the wit and the brains and the wherewithal to do that lovingly. Because I have that confidence, I'm able to just naturally and organically unfurl with them.

I heard a very similar point from Lance Mason, a nationally recognized dating coach whom we'll meet more in depth in the next chapter. For women who aren't having luck ending conversations through subtle energy and body language, as Lalla has perfected, Mason recommends practicing how to explicitly end a conversation.

MASON: When I work with men, I tend to help them on

how to start conversations. Most men are very bad at that—especially with attractive women. But when I work with women, however, I teach them how to *end* conversations. Most women are very bad at that. The reason that most women are bad at that is that they try to do it via the subtle mechanisms that other women would understand—body language, facial expressions, vocal tonality—but that men are often clueless about.

A lot of times what women will do to end a conversation is smile at a guy, but they'll give him that half-smile, with a tight jaw. In their mind, they're communicating "I'm uncomfortable, I don't want to talk to you anymore, this isn't going to go anywhere." And they assume the man can read that. But they're not speaking in his native language, so to speak.

So women need to practice—and I've worked with a lot of women on this—how to explicitly end a conversation. I'll literally role-play the creepy guy for them, who won't take a hint on ending the conversation. I'll have them practice ending the conversation explicitly. "I've got to get back to my friends." "I have to go now." They can even interrupt, if a guy is telling a long story. Just look like you've spotted some friends, extend a hand, and say "Hey, it was nice to meet you." They don't even have to explain it. It's great. They'll practice this ten times, and then all of the sudden the lights come on, because they realize, "Wow, if I can end the conversation quickly and effectively when I don't feel comfortable anymore, I can make eye contact with anyone."

That is so powerful, because if women mastered that skill, they could initiate, through their eyes and body language, so many more conversations, and be meeting so many more potential "Mr. Rights," while knowing that they can cut off the conversation when they want to.

A lot of women are understandably afraid of making eye contact with guys they may be interested in, because at some point in a woman's life, when she was younger, she invited a man to come into her space somehow, maybe just in a conversation, and he abused that invitation. And that's happened over and over again, and it's happened at every evolution in the relationship. It's happened with eye contact, it's happened with conversation, it's happened when she gave her phone number or e-mail away, she told a guy she'd meet him and then he stalked her when she didn't want to meet him again. It's happened all through her life and at all phases of her relationships, so women learn that there's a risk whenever they invite someone into their space.

So one way women can overcome this history is by practicing really good boundaries. Women need to practice boundaries *before* they practice eye contact.

Women can go to bars and not make eye contact, and they're probably still going to get asked out for a date. But they're not going to have a choice over the man who asks them out. What women will find is that when they practice their boundaries, and they open themselves up to introducing themselves to more guys with eye contact, they'll start actually having choices with the men they meet.

I talked with Annie Lalla about this dynamic.

ELLSBERG: When you are in a social setting and spot a guy you are interested in, do you intentionally make eye contact with that guy?

LALLA: Absolutely! The first thing I do is I make eye contact, and I immediately smile. I'm saying with my eyes, "Hello, I acknowledge your existence." My smile says, "I'm clapping for your existence." After that, almost unanimously, that gets met with eye contact and a smile back. They either come up to me at that point, or if I feel like it, I go up and make some engaging first comment, either about how they look, or some question that opens them up.

ELLSBERG: And it seems to me, the result of your openness with your eyes and body language was that you have a lot more choice with men than most women ever do.

LALLA: Of course I have more choice, absolutely. And, more importantly, I have a lot more mutually fulfilling interactions with humans—women and men.

Breaking All the Rules

No discussion of eye contact, flirting, and dating would be complete without consideration of the 1995 paean to manipulation, deception, and superficiality on the part of women in the name of finding true love: *The Rules: Time-Tested Secrets for Capturing the Heart of Mr. Right*, by Ellen Fein and Sherrie Schneider.

While it predates my own book by fifteen years, *The Rules* can be read as a kind of anti-*Power of Eye Contact*, its precisely diametrical opposite within the sphere of literary endeavor. So I must chime in.

One of the central axioms of the book is that letting a man know you are interested in him is roughly the romantic equivalent of puking on him on the first date. As if anticipating Eye Gazing Parties and my own book, they write:

> *[Rules Girls] don't look wildly around to catch men's eyes. They don't say hello first. . . .*
>
> *Looking at someone first is a dead giveaway of interest. . . .*
>
> *Did you know that there are workshops designed to teach women how to make eye contact with men they find attractive? Save your money. It is never necessary to make eye contact. . . . On the first date, avoid staring romantically into his eyes.*[4]

The rest of the book is filled with analogous advice, such as "Don't Talk to a Man First," "Don't . . . Talk Too Much," "Rarely Return His Calls," "Always End Phone Calls First," "Don't Speak Unless Spoken To," "Make Sure Your Burqa Does Not Expose Your Neck Flesh For His Unwholesome Temptation." (OK, I made those last two up—but I did hear they added the latter in the bestselling 2000 Kabul edition.)

What to say to all of this?

I wish I could say *it's just not effective.* But that's too simple. It probably is effective. Very effective. There are plenty of women who have driven men crazy with all this elusiveness and aloofness to the point where the man is obsessed. I've been one of those men before.

Just as there are men who have been successful luring women into bed with slick lines, rehearsed routines, and other phony gambits and put-ons.

The truth is, there are lots of insecure men *and* women out there, and it's really not that hard to get them into bed or relationships by playing on their insecurities and human weaknesses through games and artificial ploys.

I'm not posturing as a saint here or pretending to stand above all this. Rather, I know it from personal experience. I devoured *The Game,* the infamous bestselling pickup book, when it came out in 2005, along with just about every other straight male around the globe. I tried my share of pickup tricks. You know what? *It works.* Throughout my long dating career in my twenties, I behaved in many selfish, manipulative, and sometimes just plain boneheaded ways I'm not proud of looking back on. How many guys can't honestly say the same of themselves? (One day I'll distribute the tell-all . . .)

But here's the problem with all of this. Over my years of dating, in all kinds of ways—the good, the bad, and the ugly— I learned that *the way you get into a relationship presages the way your relationship will be.*

"I think 90 percent of the *The Rules* is B.S.," says Marie Forleo (www.marieforleo.com), author of *Make Every Man Want You: How to Be So Irresistible You'll Barely Keep from Dating Yourself.* "Keeping someone off balance may work as a tool for generating attraction. But you know what? It's also a tool for generating *relationships* that are off balance."

Forleo once told a *Forbes* journalist, "How you do one thing is how you do everything."[5] I wholeheartedly agree. It's very unlikely, in my opinion, that a relationship started on manipulation, deceit, game playing, and shutting out the other person will—once you've ensnared your target into a long-term commitment—suddenly morph into an honest, trusting, loving relationship. In a parallel manner, it's very unlikely that a relationship barren of open, honest eye communication to begin with will suddenly develop it, like flowers of open-heartedness blooming in the emotional desert.

Jena and I have had the pleasure of several dinners with Forleo and her fiancé, Josh, a distinguished and successful actor, who, Forleo isn't ashamed of pointing out in her blog, is certainly a catch.

How did she attract this great guy? With a bunch of elusive games and manipulations? "I spotted him and knew he was exactly the one I wanted," Forleo told me. "I made direct eye contact with him and walked up to him. And on our first date, I kissed *him*. He was shocked [giggle]."

"I say, rules shmules!" she writes in her book, which teaches women to be irresistible by being real, open, honest, and deep.

There are times when calling a man is absolutely the thing to do. Eye contact can be very sexy. Talking can be soul enlivening. Sex on the first date can lead to an intensely satisfying lifelong relationship. Dating several men can be fun and exciting.
Now there are times when these behaviors don't work and

kill your irresistibility. It's not, however, because of the "rule."
It's because of who you are being when you're calling, looking,
sexing, dating, and so on. You can break every rule in the book
when you're fully centered and self-aware.[6]

You may think I'm veering off course here with this discussion, but I think that what we're talking about here is intensely relevant to eye contact. In my experience, the biggest question most women have around eye contact as it relates to flirting and dating is not some technical question such as "How do I do it?" but rather a more fundamental one: "*Should* I do it? Isn't it too forward? Won't he think I'm easy, or desperate?" Books like *The Rules* play into millenia-old social pressure on women to be coy, aloof, and passive-aggressive in romance, not direct, open, and honest. Thus, any discussion of eye contact and dating for women needs to address these questions head on, which is what I'm doing in this chapter.

Hearing Forleo's story of how she met Josh, with no B.S. at the outset of their relationship, I was reminded of another book, *He's Just Not That Into You: The No-Excuses Truth to Understanding Guys*, the bestselling dating book by Greg Behrendt and Liz Tuccillo.

The book has been dismissed by many as a joke book, a fun and light gag, but I read it, and I actually think it shares a profoundly important message for women and men. Most relationships that actually end up working, the book argues, *work from the beginning.* They don't start with a bunch of games, deceits, ambiguities, and ploys and then suddenly turn into trusting, loving, open-hearted relationships.

The authors have a feature that runs through the book, which I think all single women and men should read: "This Is What It Should Look Like." It describes how various successful relationships started out. In one such section, Greg Behrendt writes:

My friend Mike liked my friend Laura. After band practice he
asked her out and now they're married. . . . My friend Jeff met
a girl out of town and went and visited her the next weekend
and never stopped visiting her until he moved in with her. It's
really that simple. It's almost always that simple.[7]

I go into my own story more in the next chapter, but here
I'll say that Jena and I broke *every rule in the book*. Our first date
lasted around ten hours, from 9 p.m. to 7 a.m. Our second date
was *two days* later, and two hours into it, I told her I was falling
in love with her. That's exactly what I felt, I trusted that feeling,
and I said it. She didn't play games or play coy in response. She
looked me back, right in the eyes, and said the same back to me,
straight ahead. That very date I committed to moving across the
country to be with her, and we were in a relationship *halfway into*
our second date. I picked up my life in San Francisco and moved
across the country for love, a month and a half after that.

A year later, Jena is now sporting a shiny new ring on her
left ring finger (so am I on my more metrosexual days), and
we're ecstatic about our future together.

Ladies, if anything in this chapter speaks to you, about eye
contact or anything else, my message to you is this: *Make your*
own rules.

Eye Flirting 101

Nearly every dating expert I spoke with shared a message similar to what McCann, Lalla, Mason, and Forleo are saying. Essentially, "Ladies, be proactive. If you see Mr. Right, don't wait
around passively for him to make the first move. Make the first
move yourself, with your eyes."

Janis Spindel is one of the most exclusive and renowned

matchmakers in America. Her high-powered male clients (celebrities, executives, politicians, athletes) pay her up to $500,000 to find their match. She has been featured on *Dr. Phil*, the *Today* show, CNN, in *The New Yorker*, and frequently in the *New York Times*. She is responsible for over nine hundred marriages. (Since it only takes three marriages for a yenta to earn her way to heaven, according to Jewish lore, Spindel already has several hundred extra tickets.) Though happily married with children, she is also a proud "pickup queen" herself: she hunts for many of her clients as well as many of the brides-to-be for her clients simply by walking up to them—in the first class section of airplanes, in fancy restaurants, at events—and asking if they're single. Spindel (www.janisspindelmatchmaker.com) is the author of *How to Date Men: Dating Secrets from America's Top Matchmaker* and *Get Serious About Getting Married: 365 Proven Ways to Find Love in a Year.*

I asked Spindel what a woman should do if she spots a man she's interested in.

SPINDEL: Let me tell you something. Men are intimidated by pretty women. Obviously, intimidated *and* attracted at the same time. So if a guy sees a girl who looks like her body language is not approachable, and he's attracted to her, there's not a chance he's going to go up to her at a bar, or a restaurant, or anywhere. If her body language is "I'm unapproachable, don't come talk to me," it's not going to happen.

The first thing you should do if you're in a bar and you see a guy you like is make eye contact and smile. If you make eye contact and smile, in a nanosecond he'll come over. Because that basically means "Hey, I want to meet you, I'm friendly, I'm approachable. You can come up to me. We connected in our eyes, so *buddy*, get over here now and talk to me." And if he doesn't come over, then go over to *him*.

Lauren Frances (www.laurenfrances.com) travels the world as a dating coach and relationships expert and is the author of *Dating, Mating, and Manhandling: The Ornithological Guide to Men*. She was passionate about the topic of proactive flirting and eye contact for women.

FRANCES: I teach "Man Magnet" seminars all over the country, and the first tip I teach is how to break the ice by "throwing men a crumb." This involves looking them in the eye, smiling at them, and paying them a compliment. I suggest that women do this to three new men each night they go out. If you see a guy you like, I suggest you quickly make direct eye contact, smile, and say "Nice T-shirt!" [flirtatious voice] or "Nice tie!" or "Nice watch!" Anybody you meet will be happy to get a compliment. If the guy's single and he likes you, he'll come find *you* after that! And you don't have to have further contact if it doesn't click. You can just keep walking.

That tip is gold. Women get amazing results from mastering this, and often up their odds of romantic success by 200 percent. I've heard women say, "Well, I want a guy with enough balls to ask me out." And I say, "Well, in a perfect world, the ice caps wouldn't be melting. But in the real world, men sometimes need a little nudge to know that you're actually available."

It's the most difficult thing for women to do, though. Women are trained to not look at men directly, because they think it'll be considered too much of a come-on. I call this "antiquated flirt technology." Most women still date like what I call "Sleeping Beauties in a Coma." It's totally bred into us. In fairy tales, all Sleeping Beauty had to do was spin flax and take long naps to find her dream man. Many women are still expecting their Prince Charming to rush in and save them from their lives of intense boredom. They just don't feel that they are supposed to be proactive in this area, and if they are, that it's tacky. Unfortunately, a lot of women who play "hard to get" go home alone, because they *are* hard to get, and not in the right way. The guys that you want to meet are usually the very ones who respect your personal space too much to barge in and start hitting on you when you're in a market or in an elevator. There is a kind of guy who does that, who's a hardened womanizer, and just doesn't care. He's cocky, and it's just a numbers game for him.

The great guy most women really want to meet is usually going to long for you from afar but will leave you alone until he gets a cue from you that it's OK to approach. If you keep your eyes up, scout around, and see who's in your vicinity, and then make direct eye contact and toss him a smile and a compliment, he'll happily chirp away with you. This is the secret. This is the holy grail of dating for women. The good guys need that little crumb of approval before they come in for a landing!

A lot of women are very unrealistic about how they're going to find what they want in love and dating, and don't know how to be successfully proactive about achieving their goals. If you want a career, there's usually a career path or track that most women are willing to do. But many women don't feel like they're supposed to put the same energy into creating a love life. They're still feeling that, somehow, if they put a lot of energy into it, they're desperate losers, or like its uncool and unromantic.

But a great love life is not going to magically appear for you, any more than a great career is going to magically appear. If you want to have the love life that you want, then you have to do some proactive flirting to get it. And that involves making pro-active eye contact. As a love coach, one of the biggest things I run into is that women are incredibly passive, and they're missing opportunities to meet the right one—at the laundromat, the car wash, in your veterinarian's waiting room. I always say, "Flirting beats flipping through *Cat Fancy*." I can promise you that.

Here's the thing about eye contact. Everybody wants to be seen. We live in a world where it's very hard to be seen—there's so much competing for everyone else's attention. To feel like someone is actually stopping and taking the time to see you is actually a profound experience for people. And it's almost always welcome, when it's done with a smile. It's like giving someone a little gift. It's a gracious thing to do. And it *doesn't mean more than that.* That women are still being socialized to not look at men is so archaic and obtuse in today's world. It's actually ineffective. It doesn't make people inspired to chase after you. It's actually saying "buzz off." Eye contact is just a modern way of dropping a hanky.

Be a good *lookout* for love. When you're at the supermarket, for example, keep your eyes up and signal your attraction to a man you're interested in when you're squeezing that peach.

Let down your shield, put out your welcome mat, look out at the big, beautiful world. Notice who's around you. Men are everywhere. In my book, I compare men to birds. All you have to do is look up, and there they are.

If you're reading this and still feel apprehensive about the idea of making eye contact or even approaching men you're inter- ested, Regena Thomashauer encourages you to take it step by step. Thomashauer, aka Mama Gena (www.mamagenas.com), teaches popular workshops for women on how to "use the power of pleasure to have their way with the world." A major component of the workshops is teaching women to take plea- sure in their power to flirt with men. She is the author of the bestselling *Mama Gena's School of Womanly Arts: Using the Power of Pleasure to Have Your Way with the World* and has been featured on the *Today* show, *20/20*, NPR, and the *New York Times.*

MAMA GENA: You have to cater to where each woman is. For some women—let's say she's widowed or divorced—it might be a big deal just to get to a bar. For her, she should give herself a rousing round of applause just for getting there.

Then, maybe the second time, to make eye contact with one guy she thinks is cute. She doesn't have to talk to him, just make eye contact with him, and then she's off the hook—she's done her job.

And then maybe the third time she goes out, she becomes a little more comfortable. Then make *lingering* eye contact with a guy you think is cute.

Most women think it has to do with "Am I pretty enough?" "Am I sexy enough?" But it's not that at all. It's really just skill-building. It's practicing and feeling comfortable.

Even though it involves practice, don't make it boring or get hard on yourself. The whole goal-oriented, hard-work paradigm is very boring to me. Very often it soaks the life right out of somebody.

My school is about fanning the flames of women's desires, having a woman locate what her passion is, what she wants, what she's yearning for, and to allow her innate capacity to attract those desires to surface.

There's a bit of divinity in every desire. Think of a woman yearning for an incredible guy. She's like, "Ahhh, it would be so wonderful if I met an incredible guy." She's having those thoughts, enjoying the thoughts of what it might be like to have a great boyfriend, enjoying the men she meets.

And then, "Ding!" When the right guy sees her, there's just something that he's attracted to in her. It stops him in his tracks.

That's her desire, radiating from her eyes, her whole being. She's lit up at the thought of "Fantastic guy!"

There's an enormous amount of power that human beings have, that is nonverbal, that lives in our yearnings, our longings, our desires.

If you're doing it for fun, for pleasure, you're going to get results. And if you're doing it for results, you might as well not even try.

At this point, Mama Gena's adorable dog Princess came up to me, sat at the base of the couch I was sitting on, gazed straight at me with an irresistible look, and wouldn't leave until I paid attention to her. I petted her, and she growled in delight.

ELLSBERG: *She's* a total flirt! You've trained her well to go for her pleasure [laughing].

MAMA GENA: No, *she* trains *me!* See, she's doing it right. She knows exactly what she wants, and she goes for it [laughing].

While not every woman who reads the advice of McCann, Lalla, Mason, Spindel, Forleo, Frances. and Mama Gena may be ready to walk up to attractive men and start conversations, I hope the perspectives of these experts will at least inspire women to pay more attention to how they invite or push away potential dates with their eyes. Victoria Zdrok, a Ph.D. psychologist, dating coach, and author whom we'll meet more in depth in the next chapter, put it to me this way: "With their eyes, women are always saying 'green light' or 'red light.'" Ladies, pay attention to the ways you might be saying "Red light—stay away" at times when you really might want to be saying "Green light—come over and say hi."

One of my own longest romantic relationships started when a woman gave me a "green light" with her eyes. I was sitting in a small bar in Williamsburg, Brooklyn. An attractive woman walked in, flashed me a brief smile with direct eye contact as she passed me, grabbed a drink, and sat down alone.

The effect of that one smile and gaze was overpowering for me. I had been so used to women in New York averting their gaze—standard fare for both men and women in big cities. I walked over to this woman, who had been so inviting with her eye contact, and started a conversation. Soon we started dating, and soon after that we were a couple.

My suggestion to women: if you see a guy you're interested in, don't be shy! So many women look away from men they're interested in, whether it's out of shyness, fear, embarrassment, or a more calculated desire to play "hard to get." Learning to give brief, subtle "eye invitations" to men who intrigue you will supercharge your dating life, as it did for McCann and Lalla.

FOUR

Eye Flirting, Part II

For Men Only

Glances are the heavy artillery of the flirt: everything can be conveyed in a look, yet that look can always be denied, for it cannot be quoted word for word.

—STENDHAL[1]

For the guys out there reading this:

How would you like to be in a nightclub and have a Penthouse Pet of the Year walk up to you and slip you a card with her personal phone number and e-mail address on it?

This sounds like the kind of thing that happens only in "Penthouse Letters," those salacious stories supposedly submitted by readers in each issue of the men's magazine. But it actually happened to a fellow named John in a Manhattan nightclub several years ago.

I learned of this story from the woman who slipped him the card, Dr. Victoria Zdrok, a Ph.D. psychologist (and an attorney), who also happens to be the only woman ever to be both a *Penthouse* Pet of the Year and a *Playboy* Playmate. She is the author of *Dr. Z on Scoring: How to Pick Up, Seduce, and Hook Up with Hot Women.*

ZDROK: I was on a date at the club. But I locked eyes with a different man. For the rest of the night, I couldn't think about my date or what he was saying any more. All I could think about was this other man's eyes. They electrified me, sending pulsing energy throughout my entire body.

Throughout the evening, the other man and I kept stealing brief moments of eye contact. Each time sent shivers down my spine. I knew I had to meet him. I didn't want to be rude to my date, and also, the other man was there with a date as well. So it wasn't easy. But finally, as we were leaving, I discreetly walked over to him and handed him my card, without saying a word— I just looked him deeply in the eyes as I gave it to him.

All I could think about was "Is he going to call? Is he going to call?" When John finally did call, I knew it was meant to be.

———————

It was a fateful gaze for Victoria Zdrok and John. They are now married.

ELLSBERG: Why do you think eye contact is so important to flirting and seduction?

ZDROK: Confidence is the number-one thing women find sexy in a man. And few things convey confidence in a man more than clear, direct eye contact. If a man doesn't make eye contact well, he comes across as awkward, shy, and not in his own skin. And if he does, the results are electrifying.

———————

"Your eyes are your primary flirting tools," Zdrok writes in *Dr. Z on Scoring,* aimed at men who would like to get their confidence up to be able to approach and date women as attractive as her. Men "don't realize that the content of what they say is far less important than the context in which it is said, and that their nonverbal behavior plays a far larger role in making an impression on women than the cleverness of their lines."[2] She also advises guys to pay more attention to the signals women make with their eyes.

ZDROK: Research shows that if a woman makes eye contact with you and looks away and then looks back at you again within forty-five seconds, she almost surely wants you to approach her. In my own case, when I see a guy I like in a club, I make brief eye contact with him, then look away. I might look back a few moments later and make eye contact again. If he doesn't get the point that I'd like to talk with him by then, then he's not really worth talking with in the first place.

In the year or so before I met Jena, I had become more skilled at approaching women than I ever had been in my early and middle twenties, when I used to be terrified of the prospect of approaching a woman at a club.

What changed for me? Did I all of a sudden learn a host of magic key pickup lines? Actually, most of my lines were fairly boring—things like "Hey, what's up?" or "Hey, how are you this evening?"—not exactly worthy of the Don Juan awards for poetic seduction.

How was I able to start and maintain conversations with attractive women using such dull lines? I started paying attention to the ways women make the first move with their eyes. I started approaching women who had given me a clear signal with their eyes, however brief or subtle.

I'm in no way implying that every woman in the bar or club was making eyes at me. Far from it. I just became highly attuned to and aware of the ones who were. Guys, if you pay attention, there are usually going to be a few women in any social environment who are giving you signals with their eyes. Most of us are just too boneheaded to pick up on it, so we instead try to "pick up" women who have demonstrated no interest in us at all with their eyes or body language.

I found that, as soon as I got attuned to the signals some women were sending me with their eyes, I could walk over and say practically anything (as long as it wasn't rude or offensive) to a woman who had said "yes!" with her eyes, and she would be receptive to a conversation. Once we become attuned to the radar power the eyes have for signaling interest, a whole new world opens up, and an entire level of communication we have been missing gets revealed—one that is crystal-clear yet has nothing to do with words. It's as if we suddenly develop infrared on top of our regular vision.

Lance Mason and the Art of Attraction

If you've followed the news at all in the past five or so years, you're probably at least faintly aware of the phenomenon of "pickup artists." Author Neil Strauss hilariously chronicled his descent into this underworld of men who devote themselves wholeheartedly to the art of picking up women, in his international bestseller *The Game: Penetrating the International Society of Pickup Artists* (which, as I mentioned in the last chapter, I was quite a fan of when it came out). One of the pickup artists (or PUAs, as they call themselves) featured in the book, named Mystery, went on to publish his own book and to get his own reality show on VH1, *The Pickup Artist*.

All this media attention launched tens of thousands of men into bars and clubs, including me, trying our own versions of these pickup antics, using intricate pickup lines, "routines," magic tricks, costumes, and other techniques and tricks to try to entice women into sleeping with them.

In this midst of this frenzied scene, a backlash of sorts developed. Some of us decided that we didn't want to use a bunch of tricks or prepackaged routines to attract women. We wanted to be attractive naturally, by developing the aspects of ourselves that women have always found attractive—our own inner confidence, graceful and calm body language, charm, and our own sense of playful flirtation.

One leader in this "natural attraction" movement was Lance Mason, founder of the San Francisco company ArtofAttraction .com, which teaches men how to be confident approaching and talking to women, and how to flirt effectively. Mason has been featured in *USA Today*, in *San Francisco* magazine, and on CNBC in a TV segment that also featured . . . *yours truly*.

(Mason's message that I could be attractive to women just by being myself—"the most confident, attractive version of yourself," as he put it—was appealing to me. I signed up for their intro course. CNBC happened to be filming my section and asked me if they could follow me through the course as a student. I agreed, eager for the spotlight. They titled the segment, which aired on national television, "Dating Help for Dorks," and it focused mostly on . . . *me*. You can find the segment by googling "MSNBC" and "Dating Help for Dorks." By the way, the company then had the less wholesome-sounding name PickUp101.)

As I was writing this book I caught up with Mason in San Francisco to hear if he had anything interesting to say on the topic of eye contact and dating. He gave me one of the most subtle, thoughtful, and insightful interviews on this topic during my entire research.

MASON: Guys who do study eye contact tend to do that in a business setting. And while I definitely think that's valuable, I don't think that's the only way you should study it. Because in a business setting men tend to send their power out through their eyes, projecting their power outward. They learn to project better than they learn to receive. But in the context of dating, men need to realize that they need to learn to receive with eye contact, too. A lot of guys are really uncomfortable with that.

ELLSBERG: What advice about eye contact would you give a guy who's in a bar and who spots a woman he'd like to talk with?

MASON: The most important advice is to smile. A lot of guys have been taught—make direct eye contact, more eye contact is better, don't look away. But if you do it without smiling, it freaks women out. We call it the "serial killer stare."

ELLSBERG: But here's a question—can't one go too far in the other direction? I read once that smiles evolved among primates as a submissive gesture. If one smiles too much, especially for men, isn't there a danger of appearing submissive or overly concerned with social approval? Like "Please, don't hurt me!"

MASON: This is an important issue. There's a right way and a wrong way to smile. The wrong way is to have a lot of tension in your jaw as you smile. You can actually try this yourself. Try clenching your teeth tight, and then raise your cheeks in a smile. [Mason mocked this gesture, and I recoiled instantly.]

ELLSBERG: A shiver of "Let me get away from you!" just went through my body.

MASON: That's right! [laughing]. Not only does it look creepy, it *feels* creepy. And if it feels creepy as you do it, imagine how it feels to women who are seeing it.

The right way to smile is to relax your jaw. That tells women that you're relaxed—not freaking out because you're talking with her—which is crucial.

ELLSBERG: I have always had an intuitive sense that the jaw is highly relevant to eye contact. But you're the first person

I've heard who has pointed to this explicitly. What's going on with the jaw here? Why is it so important?

MASON: The jaw muscle is the most psychologically significant muscle in the human body. (It's also the strongest.) The jaw is basically the gateway to intimate space. If I'm having a conversation about something really heavy, and I'm not wanting to deal with it, the way I'll protect myself is by keeping my jaw tense. There's something happening that I don't want to receive emotionally—I just want to receive it intellectually. The jaw is the gateway I can close to protect my emotional being from whatever is going on out in the world.

Obviously, that's not attractive to most women. Most women are more open to the world than men. As men, when we reach out to women, we want to make sure we're open emotionally. And the way we demonstrate that is by relaxing the jaw.

ELLSBERG: I know this sounds silly to ask, but how exactly do you relax your jaw? I have a lot of trouble relaxing it. I often finding myself tensing my jaw much more frequently than I'd like, and I do think it affects the quality of my face-to-face intimacy with others.

MASON: You don't pull your jaw down. You just let it drop. If your jaw is really dropped, you can hold on to your chin and move your lower jaw side by side quite a bit. If your jaw is tense, you can't do that—it's totally rigid and locked in.

ELLSBERG: But isn't there a risk here of looking like a moron or a dope?"

MASON: Look through magazines. Wherever there's a magazine where people are supposed to be happy, but they're not supposed to be sexy—like *Good Housekeeping*, for example—flip through it, and every model will smile, but they'll have a tense jaw. Now, flip any magazine where they're supposed to be sexy, like *GQ* or *Cosmo*, or really most magazines now, and you'll notice that most models—they might be smiling, or they might not be—but they all have a relaxed jaw.

ELLSBERG: I've never heard that distinction before. What does a relaxed-jaw smile look like?

MASON: It looks like a shit-eating grin! [laughing] It looks ridiculously happy. But you know what? Women love it.

ELLSBERG: Why do you think the jaw has such psychological connections?

MASON: There's an absolute, hardwired link between your emotional being and emotional state, and your physical being and physical state. It's all through the body—if my back is tense, it's going to create emotional anxiety. If my shoulders are tense, it's going to create more anxiety. And if things in my face are tense, it's going to create immediate impact.

Let's say you're in a bad mood, and I fix everything about the way you're carrying your body. It might take a couple of minutes for you to feel the effect, and it's going to be subtle. But if I put even the cheesiest smile on your face—even if I use that old trick of putting a pencil in your mouth, which forces you to have what has to be the worst smile ever—it has an immediate impact. All the muscles on your face affect your emotional state more than all the other muscles in your body combined.

The reason for that is pretty simple. Animals early on are always looking at each other's face to figure out how the other one is. The face has always been the communication center of the body. It's probably because the eyes are on the face; the teeth are on the face. And the jaw is stronger than every other muscle on the face combined.

———

One manual of body language I found, *Body Language for Dummies*, backs up Mason's view of the importance of a relaxed jaw for smiling and eye contact.

   [A smile] in which the lower jaw simply releases downwards,
   is a favorite of politicians, movie stars and celebrities. Knowing

how contagious laughter is, a person wanting to elicit positive reactions from his adoring public lets his jaw drop, suggesting playfulness and amusement. . . . Because laughter is more contagious than just smiling, the next time you're in company and want to introduce a sense of playfulness in your listeners, apply the drop-jaw smile. By looking unthreatening and as if you're laughing, the others pick up on that feeling too."[3]

However, Mason points out that—like everything else— there is a time and place for smiling. It's great for opening an interaction because it is so disarming and nonthreatening. It gets rid of all tension. Yet, if you're attracted to a woman, there's one kind of tension you *want* to build, and that is sexual or romantic tension. If you just keep smiling all the time, Mason points out, you kill any sexual tension that may be evolving.

MASON: If you're making eye contact with a woman, and then you smile, you'll notice an immediate release of tension. It's similar to laughter. If there's something tense going on—it can be a good tension or a bad tension, a sexual tension or a nonsexual tension—if there's laughter, that tension is going to escape. And if there's a smile, that tension is going to escape.

The first person who smiles, then, is choosing to release the tension. From a dating perspective, that can be a good or a bad thing. What you want to do is have control of it. A lot of times when I'm making eye contact with a woman, and she's really there, present to me, I'll *stop* smiling, because it feels right in that moment to build the sexual tension. At other times, I'll make eye contact with a woman, and it will feel like the tension is overpowering for her. In that case, I'll choose to smile.

Really what I'm trying to do is monitor the level of sexual tension. Eye contact is something that's going to increase sexual tension, and a smile will decrease it.

Another thing I've noticed is that when people are open and ready to make eye contact, they often very slightly lower their jaw, angling their face down while still looking at you. It's almost like a predator—imagine you're a lion, and you see your target prey, immediately you lower your jaw and tilt your head down. Women will do that to you, and you can do it right back. If a woman does that to you, she's inviting you to amp up the sexual tension. It's a full engagement of "We're going to embrace this sexual tension." In that situation, the last thing you want to do is dissipate the sexual tension with a smile. It's like you're ready to pounce on each other.

This happens in movies all the time. We call it the "Movie Moment." It's that moment in a movie when the two character's eyes meet, the camera slows down, it zooms in, the music and all the background noise goes silent—what the director is trying to do is recreate that moment, of total engagement of eye contact.

As soon as Mason said this, I thought of the scene in which Spencer Tracy and Katherine Hepburn first behold each other in the film *Woman of the Year*. (As I was writing this book, my father had recommended I watch this scene.)

Tracy and Hepburn were, of course, one of the most fabled couples in the history of motion pictures. They met and fell in love on the set of *Woman of the Year*. Though Tracy never divorced his wife, Louise, his main relationship for the rest of his life was with Hepburn; they remained together as lovers (with a few on-again-off-again bumps along the way) for the next twenty-five years, until Tracy's death in 1967. They filmed eight more movies together, including *Guess Who's Coming to Dinner*, for which Hepburn won her first "Best Actress" Oscar.

In *Woman of the Year*, Tracy plays Sam Craig, a no-nonsense sportswriter, and Hepburn plays Tess Harding, a high-minded political commentator, writing for the same paper. A verbal battle develops in their columns, though they've never met. Sam's editor calls him into his office. Waiting there is not only the editor but also the lithe-legged Tess; the editor wants them to call a truce.

Tess looks Sam up and down for a moment, but aside from that, their gaze does not break; it is a voracious gaze, full of the same mixture of violence, aggression, and longing that characterizes the sex act itself—at least, the most passionate, carnal, and raw incarnations of sex. Tess walks out of the room after their mutual brow beating from their editor; Sam runs after her down the hall, intoxicated . . .

Here's what's most amazing about this scene: In a very real sense, the gaze on the screen in this moment is the gaze of love. Tracy and Hepburn were introduced on the set by the film's producer, Joseph Mankiewicz. So their pairing in this scene was not only their first meeting in the movie's plot, but had to be among their first meetings in real life. We get to witness one of the great romances of the twentieth century, blooming before our eyes, in the obvious electricity and magnetism running through theirs.

ELLSBERG: Isn't it possible to have too much sexual tension, though? It can freak women out, especially in a bar when you've never met before.

MASON: Yes. It's completely up to the woman. The way I look at it, in a dating situation, the woman gets to decide how much engagement she wants. The man's job, from a dating perspective, is to create as much sexual tension as she's willing to accept, but also to always be aware of how much she's willing to accept and not make her uncomfortable.

When I'm with a woman, I want to engage her until I sense that I'm getting close to that line, or I've just barely crossed that line, or just barely started to make her uncomfortable, and then I'm immediately going to disengage.

That's a *powerful* dance. You can show a woman, "I'm going to create the sexual energy in the room, and as soon as it's too much for you, I'm going to sense that immediately, and I'm immediately going to release it." When you go through that dance two or three times—maybe with eye contact, or with conversation, or just with something innocent like touching her hand—she understands that she can trust you, and she understands that if she decides to see you more, she's safe with you. But she also knows that when she's ready for the next level, you're going to take it where she wants to go.

The really amazing thing about eye contact is that you can show her, "Hey, I'm the man you can trust. I can sense where you are. I can move things forward when you want them to move forward. And as soon as it's too much for you, you can bet that I'll notice, and I'll disengage."

ELLSBERG: So it's really about paying more attention to where the woman is at, and picking up on the subtle cues she's giving him.

MASON: Most men don't realize that the reason they're having trouble with meeting and attracting women is that they haven't been listening to women enough. They haven't been listening to the subtle ways that she gets overwhelmed with the sexual tension. Once the woman realizes, through eye contact or conversation, that you're going to respect her boundaries, that she doesn't have to fear you and put up all these artificial barriers, then all of a sudden she's like, "Of course I'll give you my number. Of course I'll go out with you." Because she knows that she's safe with you. She knows that you can read her signals.

Eye contact is a woman's first impression of how well you're able to read her comfort level, and also how well you're able to increase the sexual tension *within* her comfort level.

––––––––––

As with Zdrok, one of Mason's strongest pieces of advice for men regarding eye contact is to pay more attention to it, to become aware of all the signals women are giving them with their eyes.

MASON: Two people's eyes will meet, and then you instinctively look away for a second, and then you instinctively look back. This little interaction of meeting eyes with someone else, and then looking away, probably happens a lot more than you're aware of. It happens all the time. The reason is simple. You're strangers; there's no context for you to be having eye contact, so there's a strange tension. But, once this tension is gone, if the two people are interested in each other, they'll look back again.

At that point, if you look away from the woman a second time, you've basically given up the interaction. Remember, you have two jobs—to feel out her boundaries and respect them, and also to increase connection if you sense that's where she wants the interaction to go. If she looks back at you, she's said very clearly that she's interested in the connection going further. It doesn't necessarily mean she wants to be physical with you, but it does mean she'd at least like to have a conversation.

If you look away at that point, you've communicated a couple of things. You've communicated that for some reason you're not able to increase the connection, mainly because you're insecure. It tells her you're not totally comfortable or confident. That's not a turn-on for most women. It's certainly not a turn-on for the most confident women.

ELLSBERG: So if she looks back again, that's a good time to walk up to her and introduce yourself?

MASON: Absolutely. For me, eye contact is the best way to meet women, because there's no ambiguity about "Is she interested in me? Is she comfortable with me?" People can't fake that through their eyes. You can't pretend to feel comfortable when you're not.

If you're just walking around in your daily life, and you notice your eyes meet with a woman, and you get that chance to look away—at that point, I focus on my body, and in that split second of looking away, I think "I'm going to make the intention of connecting with this woman." I look back at her, relax my jaw, breathe in, and meet her eyes again, and walk toward her.

Here's the brilliant thing about this. Guys are always wondering, "What's the best pickup line? What's the best pickup line?" Well, if you meet her with your eyes and she meets you with hers like this, you don't need a pickup line. "Hi, I'm Michael . . . ," or "Hi, I'm Lance . . ." or just "Hi," is plenty. I assume there's already a connection, because there is, in a way. You know there's already chemistry; you know there's already mutual interest. I just walk up to a woman and extend my hand.

What Mason is describing and training his male students to become is in some sense precisely what women are constantly saying they want in a man: the *sensitive* man—who's *not* a wuss, either. The man who takes the lead, takes control of the situation, yet with exquisite sensitivity and a finely tuned receptivity to how the woman is feeling and what she desires out of the interaction. The strong, sensitive guy never fails to be a favorite among romance novel heroes.

The Decade-Deferred Kiss

I'm going to admit something embarrassing. I had a crush on one girl for ten years. One decade. The majority of my adult life up until that point. I'll call her Melissa, and she lived in my freshman-year dorm at college. She was gorgeous, and one of those people who—it was obvious, even as she sat in Economics 101—was destined for greatness (which she has since achieved, in business.)

At that time, age eighteen, my idea of how to attract a woman was to be a puppy dog. "Oh, you need help with your computer? No problem, I'll come right down and help out. Oh, you want someone to critique your speech for class? Great, when and where shall we meet?"

Needless to say, all this bum-kissing landed me straight in the "friend" category, without a molecule of romantic or sexual attraction on Melissa's part. One time, as we were both visiting the Bay Area over freshman-year winter break, I took her out on an epic San Francisco date, borrowing Mom's car for the privilege. Sunset stroll on the beach, followed by dinner at Greens, a vegetarian restaurant right on the water, followed by a movie, followed by another stroll on a secret beach I knew about.

As we sat on the secluded beach, under the moon, I leaned in to kiss her. "Michael!" Melissa said, as if I had just groped her inappropriately. "We're such good *friends*. I would never want to ruin that." And then, the dreaded words: "You're like a brother to me."

This went on throughout college, and then every year or so for a full *decade*. I wouldn't see her for a while, and then she would reach out to me at some point. I would take her out, and—hoping her affections had changed—try to kiss her, at which point I would be briskly reminded of our incredible friendship.

Well, ten years into our friendship, after a period of not having seen her for a while, Melissa called out of the blue. She was in New York for a conference and needed a place to crash. Could I put her up on my couch for a few nights?

Ahem . . . but of course!

That night I cooked her an elaborate meal. But this time, I had a new weapon in my arsenal . . . *eye gazing*. I had just become interested in it through my experience with salsa dancing. And I had just read an article about it on the Internet, suggesting that this was an excellent activity on a date.

"I just read about this incredible thing called eye gazing," I told her. "Basically, we sit close to each other, and look deeply into each other's eyes, without talking. The eyes are the windows of the soul, so this allows us to look right into each other's souls."

"That sounds amazing," she said.

We sat next to each other on the couch. The after-dinner ambience was just right, and we began the gaze.

This was probably the first time I had ever looked into Melissa's eyes for more than a second. Deep brown pools of warmth.

I felt a buzzing inside of me, all around me. The energy between us was palpable. And I don't think I was just making it up, because her expression looked rapt and entranced—certainly not an expression I was used to seeing on her face in relation to me.

Within a few minutes, the energy felt unbearable, as if the room was going to go down in flames. There was only one escape valve for this energy, one place it could go. Our bodies collided, like two magnets held apart for years.

I had waited ten years for that kiss. It was one of the most memorable moments of my life. (Melissa and I ended up dating for a little while, though things didn't work out between us. She is now happily married, and we're still friends.) That experience was definitely a factor in inspiring my idea for Eye Gazing Parties.

Years later, long after the initial buzz of Eye Gazing Parties had passed, I had my second mind-blowing personal experience with eye contact as it relates to interpersonal attraction.

I walked into a crowded New York City salsa club in May 2008. I was there for a night of dancing with a woman named Jena la Flamme, whom I had met briefly the year before at the Burning Man arts festival in Nevada. She had given me her card at that time, but we lived on opposite coasts (I had moved back to San Francisco and she lived in New York), so I didn't pursue her then. Now I was visiting other friends in New York and thought of her, so I called her up.

I spotted Jena in a bright red Indian-print outfit—a splash of brilliant color in a sea of black.

We greeted in between salsa tunes. The club was so loud that any conversation beyond "HOW ARE YOU DOING?" shouted close into ears was impossible. Which meant there was only one way to communicate: on the dance floor, and with our eyes.

As the salsa tune picked up speed, our eyes met. Jena's whole body was moving, but all I could pay attention to was her eyes—they pierced me. I saw compassion, longing, loss, warmth in her eyes—the whole spectrum of humanity, in two small but infinitely deep pools.

Colors swirled around us, laughter, hollers from the crowd—but there was only us together, our eyes unable to separate. Occasionally a smile eased the tension, but mostly we were rapt in each other's presence. The boundaries between us felt porous; we were one pair of lungs, gasping for breath as we shook furiously through the crescendos of the Afro-Cuban rhythms. The only thing keeping us from spinning into chaos was the ray of magnetism between our eyes, holding the tumult around us at bay as we took refuge in each other's wide gaze.

"Who is this woman?" I wondered.

I suggested we grab tea afterwards. We ended up staying

up talking until 7 a.m., sharing our life stories, our dreams and desires.

Soon after that, we became a couple. I moved across the country to be in the same city as her. After a year of a loving relationship, as we were looking out at the sunset from the Brooklyn Bridge, I got down on one knee, held a ring in front of her, and—in the most dramatic instance of eye contact in my life—looked her straight in the eyes and asked her if she would marry me.

"Yes!" came back the enthusiastic response; tears streamed down our cheeks.

It all started with a gaze, one year before.

Eye Gazing on a Date

WARNING: DO NOT TRY THIS ON A DATE UNLESS YOU WANT THE EROTIC TENSION BETWEEN YOU TO INCREASE VIOLENTLY.

I've already told you the story of how this technique thawed a freeze between me and one woman and led to a kiss for which I had waited ten years. I've also told you how it played a part in finding my life partner. Now, I'm going to tell you how to use this technique yourself.

The technique itself is rather simple. What requires some thought are the circumstances in which you do it. This is a powerful technique, and if you do it too early in the date, it could be incongruous—you barely know the person, and already you are evoking intense emotional and sexual responses. Of course, in Eye Gazing Parties strangers make intense eye contact right away. But they are at an event specifically designed for that, so—while it may be insane—at least it's a collective insanity, and there's cover in numbers.

On a date with just you and one woman, you may want to rush into whatever will amp up the erotic tension on that date right away. But I think that is a mistake. I think it is much better to save this technique for later.

Why? Because by that time, you'll have some context. You'll know each other a bit better. You'll have some sense of *why* you are already attracted to each other. On a date, this technique is a crescendo and a climax. To introduce it before its time doesn't do it justice.

All of this assumes, of course, that the date is going reasonably well, by which I mean that it's obvious to both of you that there is a chemistry and attraction between you. Why do I say that? Isn't eye gazing supposed to *create* attraction? Wouldn't it be precisely the thing called for if the date is going poorly, a kind of dating Hail Mary pass?

In my experience with eye gazing, what I have found is that it doesn't necessarily *create* attraction. What it does do, faster than any other technique I've ever found, is *reveal* attraction and make both parties unmistakably aware of it.

What that means, on a practical level, is this: Take two people who are not at all attracted to each other. Get them to gaze at each other's eyes for a few minutes, and what happens? They might feel closer, they might see each other's humanity more clearly. But I doubt that they will feel any more attraction for each other than when they started.

However, take two people who are already feeling a certain amount of attraction for each other. Get them to eye gaze, and a whole world will open up to them. What was before a slow simmer might now be a raging boil. They may see sides of the other person they hadn't noticed before—the other's vulnerability, emotions, inner pain and joy—and find all of that just as sexy, if not more so, than the external features that were more noticeable right away. Eye gazing is a catalyst to attraction. But for a catalyst to work, there already needs to be some chemistry.

What accounts for this dynamic? I believe that eye gazing allows us to see the emotional essence of a person in immediate, full-screen, high definition, high resolution. Usually, when we are already attracted to someone, our subconscious is already picking up on some of that essence. Eye gazing makes it plain as day.

So all of this goes to emphasize: If you're not feeling any reciprocal attraction between you and your date, then don't count on eye gazing to save a date that is going poorly anyway. If, however, you are already feeling a good vibe between you and your date, then suggesting eye gazing could be just the thing you need to take your connection to the next level.

It's not just my own intuition and my experience with Eye Gazing Parties that suggest this technique is effective. Believe it or not, science has chimed in as well. Arthur Aron, a psychologist at Stony Brook University, had opposite-sex strangers do several tasks together in a room. Some couples were instructed to gaze deeply in each other's eyes for two minutes. The couples who did the gazing reported significantly more attraction than the couples who didn't.[4]

Watch out, though—you're playing with fire! One of the couples from the study went on to marry.[5] It is infrequent indeed in the annals of science that a psychology lab becomes a breeding ground for marriage, but such is the power of eye gazing. "The single strongest most common indicator in accounts of falling in love is eye contact," Aron told researcher Ada Brunstein, referring to another study he conducted. Aron found that "our eyes connected" was a major theme in stories couples told of how they fell in love.[6]

If you're ready to eye gaze on a date, what do you do next? Well, in the course of any date, there's always that moment, perhaps a few hours into it, when the question, "What should we do next?" arises. Maybe after dinner, or after you've had a drink or two at the bar where you met.

Now is a perfect time to suggest eye gazing. I don't mean to plug myself here, but I actually do think a good way to bring it up is to mention that you were reading about it somewhere. (You don't need to mention where specifically.) "Hey, I was reading this book about eye contact, and it was really interesting. It said that if two people who don't know each other that well simply sit and gaze into each other's eyes for a few minutes, without talking, they can actually see aspects of the other person's soul and personality that would never show from just talking alone. Do you want to try it?"

If your date is at all adventurous, the answer will be an enthusiastic "Yes!" (If your date says "No," either she's shy and cautious, she thinks it's really weird, or she's *just not that into you*.)

Once you've got your date on board, pick a nice place to gaze. Standing in line or under neon lights is not a great place. Sitting together at a dinner table, a bar, or better yet a secluded corner in a bar, is ideal. (You may very well find yourself in a heated kissing session right after, so plan accordingly!)

Then just remind your date, "OK, we're not going to talk, we're just going to gaze." Then, dive in! Both of you will giggle, almost surely. But soon after the giggles die down, you will most likely find yourself in a state of deep trance, connection, and fascination with your date.

All the basics about eye gazing still apply. Focus on one of your partner's eyes at a time—though of course you can switch. Breathe. Let your thoughts pass gently without getting too caught up in them.

Once you're in a flow of gazing with your partner, you might try a technique that will bring the gaze to an absolute boil: *Start seeing in your partner that which she most wants to be appreciated for, and in your mind start honoring that part of her.*

All of us, of course, want to be appreciated for some superficial things—we want people to think we are beautiful, or stylish, or smart, or successful. That's not what I'm talking about here. What I'm suggesting is that you dig a layer deeper, and imagine what your date *really* wants to be appreciated for— that which he or she longs, in the deepest place in his or her heart, to be seen, recognized, and appreciated for. Usually, this deepest wish has nothing to do with external looks or rewards in life, but rather with the quality of our heart, our capacity to love, our capacity to empathize with another person and care, and our ability to bring joy, stability, happiness, and growth to another person's life.

I'm not suggesting you *assume* that these are what your date most deeply desires to be recognized for. I'm suggesting you *look* into her eyes and find out! The eyes are, after all, the windows to the soul. Look into your date's soul and find out what's there! Find out what he or she is longing to be appreciated and recognized for deep inside, and then appreciate and recognize it.

Once you are into this and are doing it, you should be feeling a noticeable rise in the connectedness and attraction between you. You might even be feeling a state of bliss, ecstasy, or complete rapt attention.

You may also, at this point, be feeling a strong desire to jump your date's bones! Guys, this would be a good time to lean in gently and slowly—keeping the eye contact until the last moment—and grace your date's lips with a kiss. Ladies, if you're wanting him to kiss you, well—do some of those things you do so well to indicate that! Smiling, cocking your head back to the side a bit, holding his hand. If he doesn't get the picture, he's a dolt!

Guys, if you do lean in for a kiss, and she doesn't reciprocate, don't be crestfallen. Just smile and go back to the gaze. A rejection in the kiss doesn't necessarily mean "No, never." It often means "No, not yet." Jena rejected my first attempt at a kiss. Then we talked for about six hours straight, about our lives, sharing the deepest parts of our hearts. To my surprise, after all that talking, she sat on my lap and kissed *me!*

At Eye Gazing Parties, people often marveled at how it was possible for people who had never met to spend *two minutes* gazing into each other's eyes without talking.

Well, how would you like to spend an entire *week* making silent eye contact with a new partner as a way to get to know him or her? This is how Chris Attwood began his relationship with his wife, Doris, to whom he has now been married for four years. Attwood is the author of the *New York Times* bestseller *The Passion Test: The Effortless Path to Discovering Your Destiny*, which he wrote with ex-wife and business partner, Janet Bray Attwood.

ATTWOOD: I met my wife online, and she was living in France at the time. I was living in California. It took about a year and a half for me to convince her that I should come over and meet her.

In my spiritual practice, it has been my habit to take silence the first week of every year. I just go someplace where it's easy to take care of food and basic necessities, and meditate inward for a week. For me, it's a great way of preparing for the new year.

Well, we agreed that I would come over and meet her for the very first time ever after Christmas. Because she also had a similar meditation background, and had been introduced to this idea of taking silence, we agreed that we would do this week together.

I flew over on December 27th, she met me at the airport, and we went to her parents' house for two days. Then we spent a day on the train and ferry getting to an island off the coast of northern Germany. We had one more day talking to each other—four days total.

Then we spent a week in silence. *Talk about eye contact!* This was the extreme version of it. We had no choice but to communicate through our eyes.

What I can report is that this was the most wonderful, most phenomenal, most incredible way to begin a relationship.

Obviously, it's not for everybody! [laughing].

We had been interacting for a year and a half, by phone and e-mail, so we felt very close already. When we met each other, we felt an immediate attraction. Yet, as in any first meeting, we both felt nervousness as well. Doris in particular felt a fair amount of uncertainty.

Without the words, all you're left with is the raw emotion, just feeling it. When I encountered the uncertainty without the words to cloak it, it opened my heart. My natural response was to feel compassion, because you know what it feels like to feel uncomfortable, to feel nervous and not sure of what's going to happen.

Sometimes words have a tendency to make things more confusing, less clear. Instead of cloaking our emotions with a lot of words, by just being together, and having the eye contact, we connected and felt bonded in an extraordinary way.

Over the years, I have thought a lot about why I am so obsessed with the concept of eye contact.

One day it struck me: *I exist because of a single moment of eye contact!*

The year this book is published, my parents will celebrate their fortieth wedding anniversary. Throughout my thirty-two years, my mother has so often repeated the story of how she fell in love with my father, Daniel, that I know it by heart:

PATRICIA ELLSBERG: I had met your father briefly before at a party. A few weeks later, your aunt Jacqueline was throwing a dinner party, so I invited him to join us.

He had to work late that night, but he agreed to come after work.

When the doorbell rang, I knew it was him, because the dinner was in full swing, and he was the only one who hadn't arrived yet.

Jackie had these sunken floodlights by the front door. And when I opened the door, the light sparkled in his blue eyes.

I gasped and almost shuddered backwards—the intensity, the vividness in those eyes! An electrical current went right through my heart.

I had never felt anything like it before.

We went on our first date that weekend. By the end of the weekend, we had fallen madly in love.

FIVE

The Eyes Are the Windows to the Sale

Eye Contact for Sales and Business

B ody language is 80 percent of sales," says Victor Cheng, a successful Silicon Valley business coach who has been featured on Fox News, on MSNBC, and in the *Wall Street Journal*. Jena and I visited him as clients for help with growing Jena's weight loss coaching business.

He should know. Not only did he manage to sell us on an expensive half-day coaching session (which we were very happy with), but during the session I noticed something extremely interesting, unique, and brilliant about his awareness of body language.

Throughout the session, Cheng (www.victorcheng.com) was exquisitely attuned to Jena's body language as he proposed various angles and tacks she could potentially take for her business.

"What do you think of that idea?" Cheng asked her, in response to one angle he was proposing she take for speaking about her services to her prospective clients.

"Well, it's . . . OK," Jena said in response.

"You hate it!" Cheng said with a smile.

"Why do you say that?" she protested, having spoken nothing of hatred.

"It's written all over your body. There was no excitement in your body when I mentioned that idea."

Later in the session, in response to a line of inquiry Cheng proposed, Jena came up with an idea for a book title, *The Animal Instinct Diet*, about how we can lose weight by trusting our own bodies—our "inner animal," as Jena puts it—to guide us toward healthy ways of eating.

"That's it!" Cheng exclaimed.

"You think that's a good marketing angle?" I asked him.

"What I think is irrelevant. I can tell Jena loves it. Her eyes lit up when she said it. Her whole posture and presence changed to one of engagement and excitement. It's written all over her body that she believes in this concept, and for that reason, she's going to be very effective in talking about it to others. That's the essence of sales, right there."

I was intrigued by how much body language and eye contact figured into Cheng's coaching and his concept of sales, so I caught up with him later to ask him more about this. Cheng used to be a consultant with McKinsey & Co, one of the most prestigious consulting firms in the world, but he left to help entrepreneurs and small business owners like me and Jena get our businesses humming.

ELLSBERG: What is the relevance of eye contact to sales?

CHENG: Eye contact allows people to know subconsciously whether or not they ought to trust you and listen to you further. If you meet someone and they're talking to you and they can't look you in the eye, you subconsciously know that something is not right with the conversation. You may not be able to articulate specifically what's wrong, but you'll just know something is off. So it's very critical early in a sale.

ELLSBERG: There seem to be two main schools of thought around sales and body language. One says, "It doesn't matter what you're selling and whether you believe in it or not; you can ape the body language of someone who believes in their product and make the sale." The other says, "You can't fake this stuff. You've got to believe in your product, and if you don't, it will show in your body language." I take it you're way in the latter camp. . . .

CHENG: That's exactly right. You can take someone who is very bad at sales from a formal sales training standpoint, but is wildly enthusiastic and really believes in their product, and they will be very effective in sales. People will pick up on the enthusiasm and certainty.

If somebody invented the cure for cancer—say they spent thirty-five years of their life finding the cure—and now their problem was convincing others to take it, that person would likely be very effective in talking about this cure, even if they were a Ph.D.-super nerd without very good people skills, and even if they had no sales training at all.

If some mother whose child was saved by this drug was trying to convince a friend, whom she cares deeply about, on why they ought to take this life-saving cure, she could sell it, no problem. Even if she botched every standard sales rule you could think of. Because the conviction and enthusiasm are there. People read that.

The challenge is, most salespeople out there don't really care about what they're selling—a lot of them don't really believe in it. As customers, when we see that, we may not be consciously aware of it, but we don't buy it, because we sense something is off.

ELLSBERG: There's a lot of talk about "professional managers" who could manage any company in any industry with their universal management knowledge. In the same way, there's a notion of the "professional salesman" who could sell anything to anyone. What you're saying goes against the idea that a good salesperson could be an effective hired gun for anything. . . .

CHENG: From a business owner's standpoint, I want someone who's effective. And from experience, I know that if they think the product is crap, they're not going to be effective. They can try to fake it and pretend—and some people are actually good enough to get away with that—but they just won't feel very whole or fulfilled.

I've done that before. When I was just starting out, I sold things I wasn't terribly proud of, though I never would anymore no matter how much money was involved. It's just not fun. People can tell, and it shows up not only from a qualitative/intuitive standpoint, but in the numbers as well. I think it's terribly important to really believe in what you're selling. That enthusiasm carries across, and then you don't have to worry about technique, in terms of body language or eye contact. Your body language and eye contact will naturally show that you believe in the product.

ELLSBERG: So what do you do if you *don't* honestly think your product is right for your client? Do you just tell them that? It's hard to walk away from a potential sale. . . .

CHENG: I do that all the time. See, sales people have it rough. The assumption is, when you walk in the door, you're lying—mostly because so many people who have come before you have done that. Anytime you can do something that is contrary to being purely out for their money, it bumps the trust level up. So you can say something like, "Listen, of the three problems you talked about, the first one, honestly I can't solve. It's just not within our capabilities, we're not a good fit, and here are two or three companies you might want to look at who are pretty reputable around that issue."

So their first response is, "OK, cool—he's actually considering what's best for me," and the prospect will deeply appreciate that. Then you can continue, "The second problem you mentioned—we are the *best* solution for that. Let me explain why." They are much more likely to believe you. We did that at McKinsey a lot. If it's a problem we couldn't solve, we were usually very up front about that. I do it to this day—if someone is a better fit for them, I usually refer them. It's especially important if your expectation is that you plan to do business with this person for a long time, which is always my approach. Doing right by them early will pay off for years, and in some cases decades.

───────────

Even though Cheng says body language is 80 percent of sales, I realized while talking with him that his approach is much deeper than simple body language and eye contact "tips and tricks." It's about being deeply honest with your prospect, about your own enthusiasm for the product, and your best, good-faith estimation of whether what you're offering can help them or not. Getting those things right is the message; good body language and eye contact are just the mediums of the message. And they're powerful mediums, because they're hard to fake.

ELLSBERG: What about the eye contact and body language of the prospect? That seems just as important to pay attention to as your own body language in a sales situation.

CHENG: Most people, when they think of body language and sales, they think of the body language of the seller, trying to convince the buyer. As a professional seller, however, you also need to read what the prospect's body language is. This is stuff most people get a sense of starting in kindergarten—people fold their arms when they're unhappy. If they were smiling and now they frown, that wasn't good, and so on.

It's just the same in a sales situation. People will tell you what they like and don't like with their body language. You can tell when they're interested in a line of reasoning you've proposed, or even if they're ready to buy, long before they say anything verbally about it.

ELLSBERG: How so?

CHENG: There are some specific patterns to look for. Say you're talking to someone, or presenting to them, and they're leaning back, folding their arms, and not making good eye contact, which suggests some skepticism and disengagement. At some point, if they perk up, lean forward, and unfold their arms, and make more eye contact, that means they're engaged and open. When you see that, you've either deliberately or accidentally stumbled upon something they really care about. So when you see that reaction, you want to think to yourself, "What did I just say?" Because it was the right thing, and you want to pursue that line further.

———

Only days after I had this conversation with Cheng, I was in a meeting with a potential client who was possibly interested in hiring me to write a sales letter for his own client list. We were discussing various options, and while he wasn't looking away, or looking down, I didn't detect a lot of interest either. Then, I hit across one point—the possibility of upselling his clients to an expensive three-month coaching program—and the reaction couldn't have been clearer. He sat upright in his chair, leaned forward over his desk, and began looking me straight in the eyes as I talked.

With Cheng's distinctions fresh in mind, I knew I had

struck a chord with my potential client. I kept developing the coaching upsell idea with him, and a few minutes later, before I asked him for the sale, he leaned forward even more, looked me right in the eye, and said, "OK, Michael, how can we make this happen?" I told him my rates, and the sale was closed—without any fancy "closing" tricks or techniques. Without paying attention to his subtle body language clues, I'm not sure I would have developed that upsell theme more, as it wasn't the original idea I had come in with. I probably wouldn't have gotten the sale. (Thanks, Victor Cheng!)

ELLSBERG: What about the other situation, though—when you can't get the customer to make eye contact, and their body language is disengaged and disinterested?

CHENG: I just call them out on it. Most others don't do that. But I say, "Listen, I can tell from your body language you're not thrilled with what we're talking about. It's obvious to me you have some concerns. May I ask what those concerns are?" At that point, because you're so open about it, it's hard for them to fake it. Otherwise, they're checked out, disengaged, and just being polite with their answers.

ELLSBERG: What else should readers keep in mind about eye contact in selling situations?

CHENG: When you're in a sales meeting, either with a group or one on one, pay a lot of attention to how the chairs are arranged. This is very important, and it's almost always overlooked. If you are sitting face to face, directly across from a prospect, and making eye contact that way, it's the traditional posture or body positioning of an interrogation. It's confrontational, and it invites the frame of "One person is talking, one person is resisting."

It's much better to get them to be on the same side of the desk, or the same side of the conference table, so rather than being 180 degrees away, you're 30 degrees away. So you're look-ing over your right shoulder, and there they are. You're on the same side of the table, and you're both slightly facing toward the table, usually looking at something, like a presentation. So rather than interrogating and being interrogated, you're col-laboratively assessing an opportunity and determining whether it's a good fit.

Along the same lines, let's say you bring three people and they bring three people—it's better if it's not "You sit on one side, we sit on the other." That's confrontational again. Better to get there early and deliberately mix it up. Spread your own group around the table, so that the buyer's group then comes in and grabs their chairs around the table mixed in as well. Now you're one group, not two opposing teams.

Also, in a multi-person selling situation, such as a husband and wife, or a small group meeting with three or four poten-tial clients—who you make eye contact with conveys who you think is important. Say a husband and wife come onto a car lot, and the salesman immediately starts making eye contact with the husband and never looks the wife in the eyes. If the car is for the wife, that sale is shot.

Same deal in a meeting—if you have a senior-level person and a junior-level person, don't make the assumption that the senior person is the only one you need to impress. Make sure you balance eye contact with all the people in the room, espe-cially if you don't know who's got the power and the influence. It's not always based on title. Oftentimes, in fact, it's negatively correlated with title.

In relation to this last point about making sure to make eye contact with everyone in the room, Neil Rackham told me a story of eye contact gone terribly awry. Rackham is the author of *SPIN Selling,* widely regarded as one of the most influential and important sales books ever written. It is perhaps the only

sales book to be based on direct observation of tens of thousands of live, in-field sales calls.

RACKHAM: I remember studying a major presentation
to the board of a big public company. This was a presentation
being done by a consulting company. They were very nervous,
because many many millions of dollars in fees were resting on
this presentation.

As usually happens, to have gotten that far, and to be presenting to the board, they had to have an internal sponsor. It
happens almost all the time.

The speaker who was making the main presentation not
just made eye contact but literally *locked* eyes with the internal
sponsor. And the sponsor was happy and friendly and supportive, and nodded.

And the result was, the presenter did not see that the chair-
man of the board and the CEO were both starting to look uninterested and bored, as though he was going on too long. All
the time, he was looking at his sponsor—who was nodding and
smiling—and feeling as though he was doing a great job. The
sale died after that meeting.

Not Too Hot and Not Too Cold

Sales trainer Tony Alessandra, author of sales classics *Non-
Manipulative Selling* and *Collaborative Selling* (www.alessandra
.com), told me a story about a client of his.

ALESSANDRA: I was doing a consulting job for a name-
brand big-box retailer. And this company had what they called
the "Three Feet Rule." It meant that if a customer got within
three feet of an employee, the employee had to smile, make eye
contact, and ask "How can I help you."

Well, believe it or not, customers had been complaining about the eye contact part of it, actually leaving comments in the comment box. It turned out that *every employee* interpreted "make eye contact" differently. Some made eye contact and never broke it, drilling a hole through the customer with Superman laser eye beams. Others touched eyes for a millisecond and then never looked back.

All the employees had to be trained in proper eye contact for a salesperson.

ELLSBERG: OK, the million-dollar question. What is proper eye contact for a salesperson?

ALESSANDRA: Intermittent. You definitely want to have solid eye contact. But you should be wary of overdoing it, just as you should be wary of underdoing it.

While you might expect, in a book on eye contact, that I'd advocate making as much eye contact as possible all the time, the one thing I heard again and again from business people and sales professionals is that—in a business context particularly—you want to be just as careful of overdoing eye contact as underdoing it.

Bert Decker (www.bertdecker.com) expresses this point eloquently in *You've Got to Be Believed to Be Heard: The Complete Book of Speaking . . . in Business and in Life!*, one of the most successful and influential books on public speaking ever written. He distinguishes "involvement"—a healthy engagement with the eyes—from "intimacy" or "intimidation," both of which are the result of too much eye contact.

He writes in his book:

> *Intimacy and intimidation both involve looking at another person steadily for long periods—say, ten seconds to a minute or more. In business and normal social conversations, both intimacy and intimidation make listeners feel uncomfortable. But over 90 percent*

*of our business and social communications call for involvement.
How do you achieve that "just right" level of eye connection that
conveys a feeling of involvement? . . . A feeling of involvement
requires about five seconds of steady eye contact. That's about the
time we take to complete a thought or sentence.*[1]

To get a sense of eye contact done well and botched hor-
ribly, Decker offers the wonderful suggestion to try watching
television news with the volume turned off, while paying attention to eye contact. You'll see exactly what works, what looks
awkward, and what makes you trust or distrust the speaker.
"Look for signs of confidence and believability. See how eye
communication can enhance or betray a person's credibility
and likeability."[2]

Eye Contact for Networking

One evening, I was at a networking party in which a lot of
heavy hitters from my industry, publishing, were in attendance.
I had a mental list of all the people I wanted to talk with there.
I became more and more frantic as I angled and maneuvered
about so that I might get a chance to connect with one or more
of them and trade business cards.

I was having no luck, and my morale was going lower and
lower as I couldn't find anyone at all to talk with at all, heavy
hitter or otherwise. Soon, I seemed to be the only one in the
room standing without a conversation partner. I started feeling as though I was walking around with a big sign on my
head that said "I Am At This Networking Event Alone. I Am
a Loser. Please, Anyone, Talk with Me! By the Way, Would
Anyone Like to Do Business with Me?"

I was about to leave the event when a voice in my mind said
"Stop!" I heard this voice within me say, "Michael, your entire

energy at this event has been all about what *you* can *get* from other people. Why don't you start thinking about what you can *give* to other people?"

"What I can give to other people? What could I possibly give to other people at this party?" I argued with myself (yes, I do such things. Fortunately for my public image, I do it without moving my lips). "These are all big shots. What would they possibly want from *me?*"

"Think about it and figure it out," the voice said, and slammed a door in my consciousness shut.

"Hmmm . . ." I thought. "What could I give to other people? What might they want from me?"

I decided: before I leave this party, for five minutes I am going to walk around without a single thought of getting anything from anyone. I'm just going to ask myself the question, of whomever comes in my way—whether he or she is a useful connection to me or not: "What can I give this person?"

The next moment a man crossed my path, the kind of man whom I probably would have looked right past in my previous frantic mental state, as he didn't appear particularly powerful or connected. I looked at him and asked myself, "What could I possibly give this man?"

Instantly, the thought popped in my mind: "I can give him love."

I know it sounds extremely hokey. Please don't bring out the violins, though. I was not talking about romantic love or deep personal love. I meant the simple kindness and warmth that one human being can accord another, just because we're both alive.

I looked this man in the eyes, saw his humanity, and imagined myself sending him a powerful burst of kindness and warmth, from my heart to his. Imagined this kindness washing all over him, cleansing him of any stress or worry he might have been feeling.

To my surprise, the man didn't shriek in horror or call the straightjacket dispensers. Rather, he smiled at me warmly as our gazes met for a moment. I walked over and extended my hand.

We had a pleasant conversation for a few minutes and went our own ways. I continued with my "What can I give this person?" question for everyone who crossed my path. Usually the answer came back to me: "I can give this person love." Which isn't actually that surprising. Is there anyone, no matter how jaded on the exterior, who wouldn't appreciate a little more genuine kindness, a little more human warmth, a little more connection, in their day?

I noticed that as I made I contact with strangers during my earlier "what can I get from this person?" mentality, people looked away instantly as our eyes met. And who is to blame them? My gaze must have said "This guy wants something from me" loud and clear.

Now, I had genuinely rid myself of any conscious desire to get anything from anyone. And I hadn't just adopted the mentality "Oh, if I'm nice to people, maybe I'll get something out of it." I just decided to try an experiment: to see "how much can I give with my heart?" without a single thought of what I might get in return.

As soon as I adopted this mentality, everything shifted. Now, I met people's gaze, and they smiled. Their gaze stayed with mine. My mood was fantastic. I was getting into conversations left and right. People started coming and joining our conversations. Others begin introducing people to me within the group conversations. Everything flowed perfectly, and I left that room a changed man. The shift I experienced in that room has stayed with me, and now I engage in this practice nearly everywhere—on the sidewalk, in the subway. Whether or not anything comes of it materially, I am always in a great mood when I do it.

Oh, and lest you think this was just an airy-fairy, feel-good story with no application to business: I walked out of that party with several of the top business cards I had wanted to get, and ended up doing business with more than one of these people.

"Givers Gain" is the motto of Business Network International (BNI), the largest business networking organization in the world. I didn't have that motto in mind as I underwent my little lovefest at the networking party, but it is notable that all sources about networking I've encountered fundamentally say the same thing: networking is about *giving*, not getting. At that party, I discovered that even if you have nothing else to give, even if you give nothing but your attention, your presence, and your warmth, that is a lot, and people appreciate it and remember it.

I talked with Dr. Ivan Misner about the "givers gain" philosophy, particularly as it relates to eye contact. Misner is the founder of BNI (www.bni.com), which has 5,300 chapters around the globe and is responsible for $2.3 billion of referral business for its members each year. ("This is roughly the GDP of the nation of Liechtenstein," Misner pointed out to me with a chuckle. "Hey, it's a small country, but I think that's pretty cool.") He is the author of the *New York Times* bestsellers *Truth or Delusion?: Busting Networking's Biggest Myths* and *Masters of Networking: Building Relationships for Your Pocketbook and Soul*, and he is widely cited as "the father of modern networking."

Misner demonstrated his "givers gain" viewpoint from the first second he got on the phone with me. He is one of the most sought-after and well-connected people in the business world, with thousands of people vying for his time. Yet from that first moment he was extremely warm and friendly, generous with his time, and seemed concerned only with how best he could help my project, without a thought or mention as to how it might help him.

In response to my query about eye contact and networking, he told me a story about several times when he had met with Richard Branson, founder of the Virgin brand of companies, on Branson's private island in the Caribbean.

MISNER: Branson has this laser-focus eye contact. When he is talking to you, he's not looking to his left, looking to his right. He's giving you his full attention.

We were talking about kids and raising kids, and I was telling him about my son, who was fifteen at the time and very sharp, but not as committed to school as he could be.

Six months later, I meet Richard at this party and introduce him to my son. Branson remembered who he was, and I have this photograph of him, where he has this laser eye contact with my son, and he's talking to him for three or four minutes. All these people were around, wanting Branson's attention, but he was completely focused on my son in that moment. Branson wasn't intense in terms of his speaking—he was actually very relaxed—but he was very intense in his focus. The only person in that room, in that moment, was my son. Here's a guy who never went to college, and he was telling my son. "Go to college. I spoke to your dad! You can do better. I have faith in you!"

My son doesn't get impressed by *anybody* [laughing]. I don't think he even understood who Branson was. But I asked him afterwards, "What did you think of that conversation?" and he said "That was amazing!" He was impressed how, for those few minutes, he had Branson's undivided attention.

I've had a chance to see Branson several times now, and he's just a *master* at giving people his undivided attention. Now, when he went to the next person, he gave *that* person his undivided attention. That's one of the things that makes a *master* networker. Making others truly feel that you are interested in what they have to say. And eye contact is a key piece of that.

I run an international organization, and I meet a *lot* of people through the course of my work. One of my goals when I'm meeting people is, I want them to walk away from a conversation with me really feeling that I am interested in them and concerned about their success. And I do believe that, I feel that, I want that.

But I've met people who feel that but don't convey it. The way to convey it is to really give people focused, undivided attention. Of course eye contact is critical to that.

Undivided attention. Does this concept sound familiar? It comes up again and again in discussions with masters of connection through eye contact. We've already heard it in relation to another master networker, Bill Clinton.

Dr. Sean Stephenson, a psychotherapist, public speaker, and author of *Get Off Your "But": How to End Self-Sabotage and Stand Up for Yourself*, worked as a White House intern while in college, the summer of 1998. He writes in his book:

> *Once President Clinton's eyes locked onto yours, they didn't leave until the interaction was complete. In all my years talking to celebrities, from sports icons and Hollywood starlets to business moguls and politicians, few have used this technique with such finesse. Most of these ego-monsters can't hold the connection for more than a few seconds before they start scanning the room for someone more important to talk to than the person right in front of them. Yuck!*[3]

Mark Wiskup, a communications coach and the author of *The It Factor: Be the One People Like, Listen to, and Remember*, emphasized to me how important it is not to fall into this "look-ing for something better" mentality that many people adopt at parties and networking events, which master networkers like Branson, Misner, and Clinton avoid.

WISKUP: All of us have met someone who makes eye contact with us less than half the time. The rest of the time, they're looking for something else. I dub these people "look-past-ers." It's extremely irritating, and it ruins any connection. They could be saying the most wonderful things—about your children, about how much they enjoy your company—but if they're looking for something better, they ruin it.

The damage you do by looking past is powerful. If you see someone you really want to talk with across the room, and you're talking with someone who, for whatever reason, isn't really meaningful to you, I say have the human dignity to wait it out for another ninety seconds, give them ninety seconds of due, keep looking straight at them, be proud that you're not a "look-past-er." And when you're ready, say, "There's someone else I need to talk to, would you please excuse me?" Be official about the break, rather than giving someone half your attention and being elsewhere in the room with your other half.

It is important to remember that while eye contact *signals* un-divided attention, attention involves more than just eye con-tact. You actually do have to be *paying attention*, with all of your awareness, not just your eyes. Brian Tracy and Ron Arden write about this distinction in their book *The Power of Charm: How to Win Anyone Over in Any Situation.*

You have probably experienced the reverse of this total [at-tention]. Someone has been looking at you and very possibly making a hundred percent eye contact, but you knew "the lights were on but there was no one home." The other person was engaging in phony listening. He wasn't listening to you. His eyes had that glazed, vacant look, which immediately confirmed your worst suspicion—he wasn't really that interested in you or what you had to say.[4]

Marie Forleo referred to this same phenomenon as a "pretend gaze—their eyes are on yours, but their mind is on a Hawaiian beach."

Tracy and Arden quote a line from Elizabethan poet and statesmen Fulke Greville, which I think is spot on: "Our companions please us less from the charms we find in their conversation than from those they find in ours."

Customer Relations

Of all the experts and gurus out there on customer service, few have more experience or credibility than Jeanne Bliss, author of *Chief Customer Officer: Getting Past Lip Service to Passionate Action.*

Bliss (www.customerbliss.com) has been known as the "Chief Customer Zealot" for five major corporations. She was the leader of the Lands' End Customer Experience and the Officer for Customer Satisfaction & Retention at Allstate. She also served as Microsoft General Manager of Worldwide Customer & Partner Loyalty and as Senior Manager for Customer Satisfaction at Mazda.

I asked Bliss if eye contact is important in the customer–company relationship, and she reiterated just how crucial it is in an age when people are starved for authentic human attention, connection, listening, and presence.

BLISS: There's been a huge amount of research on the difference between hearing and listening. In customer relations, it is crucial to actively listen to what your customer is telling you, not just hear it. And while you're doing that, you always want to give cues back that you *are* listening. One of the ways you can do that is by listening with your whole body, including eye contact. I call this "unspoken feedback."

When you're giving unspoken feedback, the other person gets a sense that you have accepted and processed what they said. The truth is, none of us gets the feeling that we are being listened to that often. When someone actually listens to us, it knocks down barriers and gets us both to a soft spot, a real human connection between two people.

It's a disruption in our everyday chatter, and it has a *huge* impact on how much we trust the other person. We feel we are in a relationship, not just part of an anonymous transaction. Direct eye contact is an important part of this. It's not the only part, of course—there are so many other things that go into it—but it is an important part.

Bliss puts this another way in an article for *Sales and Service Excellence:* "We've robotized our frontline to the customer all over the world. Let them be human, give them the skills for listening and understanding and help the frontline deliver to the customers based on their needs."[5]

Since I started writing this book, I've paid a lot more attention to the quantity and quality of eye contact I experience with the frontline people of the companies I do business with: from customer service representatives to ticket agents to retail clerks and waiters. I am often shocked at how little thought or attention is paid to this area of customer relations.

It's not that difficult a concept. Look a customer straight in the eyes, and we will feel more as though you take us seriously, care about our concerns, and are sincerely curious about what is going on in our world. We will trust the company more, feel secure that they intend to build a working relationship with us over time, rather than putting us through a one-off transaction. What could be more obvious?

Yet—now that I'm attuned to it—I see poor eye contact, or no eye contact at all, at so many companies I do business with. "How is everything?" the waiter asks without looking at me. Am I supposed to believe he really cares about my experience at his establishment if he's not even looking at me when he asks?

The point here is not that I'm some kind of eye contact snob, expecting it everywhere I go. (OK, maybe I am.) The point is how remarkable and effective it is when a company gets this *right*. For years, I have been a cult fanatic of Trader Joe's, a chain of specialty supermarkets focused on the west coast and the northeast. I noticed it early on during my Trader Joe's ob-session: I always felt *good* when I left the store.

For the longest time, I pondered why this might be. And then it hit me. Not only is the staff—from the aisle stockers to the checkout to the management—preternaturally friendly, but they actually seem to honestly *care* that I enjoy my shop-ping experience there, and more important, that I enjoy the food I buy there. Of course, many things go into fostering this experience—I'm sure they have a powerful customer rela-tions training program—but one part of it is that, unlike almost every other supermarket chain I've ever been in, the employees actually look me straight in the eye when I'm talking with them. Whether they know it or not, they are practicing the "full-body listening" that Jeanne Bliss advocates passionately.

If you are a frontline employee who deals with customers directly—sales, service, customer relations, or clerk—you may think that there's not a lot extra you can do to make your cus-tomers feel *fantastic* about interacting with your company. Your company gives you protocols, and you follow them. But, you know as well as I do that if you're serious about rising through the ranks of your company, one of the best things you can do is make your customers feel *great* about having interacted with you. Some very small shifts in your quality of listening and presence can make a dramatic difference.

One of those shifts is learning to look directly at your customers when they are talking to you. It's so rare in the business world that when you do it, your customers may even be shocked with appreciation. ("Finally, someone in a corporation is listening to me!") I hope you take what I've written here to heart and try it out. Try it, and let me know what happens: michael@powerofeyecontact.com

For those of you who manage frontline employees (or who manage people who do), the fundamentals of listening to your customers with solid, direct eye contact can be taught relatively quickly. A one- or two-hour training session is probably plenty. You have all the tools you need to do this already, in this book. Can you imagine a use of two hours that would have a more high-leverage, long-term impact on how your customers feel about your company than making sure your employees are making solid, yet smart and respectful eye contact with your customers when they interact?

Job Interviews

A job interview is essentially a sales conversation in which *you* happen to be the "product" being sold, as well as the salesperson selling it.

As such, all of the standard concepts around eye contact we've been discussing so far apply. Think of all the things that eye contact telegraphs: confidence, comfort with yourself, trustworthiness, and social intelligence.

Think those might be qualities that a job interviewer will be looking for?

I talked with Dr. Paul Powers, a psychologist, about specific pointers for eye contact within the context of job interviews.

Powers is the author of *Winning Job Interviews: Reduce Interview Anxiety, Outprepare the Other Candidates, and Land the Job You Love,* one of the top-ranking job interview books on Amazon.

Powers reiterated something I have been stressing all along in this book, particularly in this chapter: With eye contact, there can definitely be *too much,* in certain circumstances, as well as too little. It's obvious, because I've written this book, that I'm an eye contact fanatic. When you are talking with me, there could never be too much. I'll lock eyes with you for 95 to 100 percent of the conversation and feel completely comfortable.

But in this realm, I'm way, way, way to the far side of the bell curve on how much eye contact I'm comfortable with. This book is not, uniformly, a book arguing that more eye contact is always better. Instead, I argue that *more effective* eye contact is always better. And part of effective eye contact is, without a doubt, gauging where the other person is and meeting them in their comfort zone. This is the "dance" we started talking about in the Introduction.

Powers, like every one else in the business world I interviewed, emphasizes this point.

POWERS: Your aim for eye contact in the job interview is what I call the "appropriate" amount. If you make the appropriate amount of eye contact, you will be viewed as confident and charming, holding the courage of your convictions, someone who can get the job done. If you don't make *enough* eye contact, you will be viewed as wishy-washy, someone who doesn't have any conviction.

And if you make *too much,* you will be viewed as overbearing, disrespectful, and overly aggressive. Don't think that the more eye contact you make, the more confident you will seem, without limit—there is a limit. You want the appropriate amount.

ELLSBERG: In your view, what is the appropriate amount, and how do you know if you're making it or not?

POWERS: The key is to check your gut. If you are at all intuitive, you'll know when you're making too much, or not enough.

———

In some ways, eye contact is a good litmus test for the general social intelligence we discussed in Chapter 1. If you don't get eye contact right, it is unlikely you'll get other subtleties of social intelligence right, either, as eye contact is such a central and telling aspect of social intelligence.

If you're really serious about acing a particular interview, Powers recommends recruiting a friend to play the interviewer, getting him or her to ask you some tough questions, and taping the interaction.

POWERS: A lot of people don't like doing it, because they don't like how they look or sound on video. Well, once we get over the fact that we don't look like George Clooney or Angelina Jolie, we can learn a lot from taping ourselves. When you are thinking about the answer to a question, do you always look up and to the right, and say "Um"? Do you look down and twiddle your fingers? Whatever you're doing that conveys nervousness or hesitation, I guarantee you won't notice it until you see it on video. But your interviewer will notice it right away.

ELLSBERG: Do interviewers consciously look at applicants' body language? Or is it more of a subconscious thing that they just pick up on?

POWERS: It's probably subconscious in most cases. But it's still one of the main things an interviewer picks up on, influencing their decision. These days, any job opening probably has many applicants who are qualified on paper. What they are looking for in the interview is a feeling, and a lot of that feeling is created through body language.

They are making a subconscious read on how comfortable you are. Do you have a laissez-faire attitude, in which you don't seem to care very much? Or are you overly rigid and tense? The interviewer doesn't want either of these. She doesn't want someone who isn't stressed out at all, but she also doesn't want someone who is extremely stressed by the interview—like, you're going to be out on the street tomorrow with no food if you don't get this job.

All kinds of studies show that peak performance occurs at a medium level of stress—not too little and not too much—and that is where you want to be: poised, alert and attentive, but not fidgety or nervous. That's what an interviewer is looking for. All of that comes through your body language and your eye contact.

Eye Contact in the Workplace

Eye contact in a business setting, particularly your workplace— where you'll be seeing people day in and day out—needs to be approached more delicately than in any other setting. In a dating or flirting situation, once you're past the initial greeting and are in a conversation, it's almost impossible to have too much eye contact. The more the better. The name of the game is connection and intimacy, and few things create that like eye contact.

But in a business setting, not only is it possible to overdo it; it's quite easy. Deep personal connection and intimacy are not only *not* prized in this setting, they're often looked upon skeptically or even cynically, in favor of cool "professionalism."

It's not my place or goal to question this reigning ethos. Rather, I'm suggesting that if you incorporate just a *little* more human-to-human connection in business settings, you will notice profound results.

Notice the italics in the word *little*. The "default" in this setting is very little eye contact at all. So if you all of a sudden go toward the deep eye gazing I suggest in the context of dating, you will be seen as a strange fruit. The key to success with eye contact in a business setting—as in all settings—is to remember that eye contact is, above all, a give-and-take.

In a business setting, you are most likely going to encounter people who are uninterested in if not downright hostile to eye contact. Rather than ramming eye contact down their face, which will get you a reputation for being a lunatic, you must meet this person right where they are within this give-and-take.

Take your typical office environment. You have co-workers all around you, some of them of higher rank, some of lower rank. You have one or more bosses. You may have several people (or a whole team or business unit) beneath you. You have receptionists, administrative assistants, and other support staff.

It's likely that most of these people have never thought about eye contact in the workplace, and a lot of them would be quite uncomfortable with the idea if you brought it up explicitly.

For that reason, I would recommend against ever *telling* anyone that you're trying to incorporate more eye contact into your experience of the workplace.

I've often noticed that I'll be talking with someone and making a nice connection with them via eye contact. Then, it will come up in the conversation that I'm writing a book on eye contact. All of the sudden, the eye contact will get strained and awkward for a little while! Usually we laugh about this, and it all goes back to normal. But it's a nice reminder. Eye contact is, above all, a process of getting out of our solitary selves and connecting with another person. If someone is unexpectedly made to feel self-conscious about it, you are no longer relating to another person but rather to your own fears, preconceptions, and worries about what the other person is thinking.

So, as you remember from Chapter 2, it is possible to make very brief eye contact with someone—a second or less—and still feel as though you have made a connection with that person. I would start this way. As you go about your day, pepper your normal conversations with just a tiny bit more eye contact than you normally would: a second here, a second there.

This can also happen within the same conversation. As you are talking with someone in your office, every once in a while during the conversation, pepper in a second or two of eye contact.

You will find that some of the people you are talking with respond well to your new eye contact. At this point, you can start introducing more eye contact into the conversation— perhaps holding now for three or four seconds. When it feels too intense, break the eye contact within the conversation.

If someone in the workplace is not receptive to your eye contact overtures, don't worry about it. Don't take it personally, and don't judge that person, either. We've all got our own comfort levels, and one of the central keys to effective eye contact is to always be aware of the other person's comfort levels.

SIX

How to Wow a Crowd with Eye Contact

Public Speaking and Presentations

If you are interested in public speaking, you have probably heard of Toastmasters (www.toastmasters.org), the largest organization devoted to helping people learn and perfect public speaking, presentation, and communication skills. The organization has 250,000 members worldwide, in 11,000 chapters around the globe.

Each year, around 25,000 of the most ambitious public speakers in the world compete in the Toastmasters World Championship of Public Speaking. The aspiring World Champions rise through a series of district and then regional competitions until only ten finalists remain, and then only one winner. Perhaps only a presidential debate is more grueling as a test of public speaking skills. These are among the best public speakers in the world (certainly better than many presidential candidates!).

I talked with several World Champions, and they all stressed the importance of eye contact to their craft. As goes without saying—in all areas covered in this book, not just public speaking—eye contact isn't the only thing. But it's an important thing, and something that has a disproportionately large impact for how easy it is to learn.

The champs I spoke with emphasized two main reasons eye contact is so crucial to public speaking, corresponding to the two directions of communication—from speaker to audience, and from audience to speaker.

Ed Tate, the 2000 World Champion and now a successful professional public speaker and trainer (www.edtate.com), feels eye contact is so important to public speaking that he begins all of his talks with a few moments of eye contact with audience members.

TATE: One mistake a lot of speakers make, including experienced professional speakers, is to start talking right away. For some speakers, not half a second passes between the time he's introduced and the time his mouth opens. That's a huge mistake, because it misses a fantastic opportunity for connecting with your audience right away.

When I get on stage, I don't start right away. I stand in front of the podium and find the center of the earth—I get really grounded, in my feet, my body. I'm just *there*. While I'm doing this, I look many people in the eyes. If it's a small seminar audience, I might be able to connect with everyone personally. If it's a larger audience, it might just be a few people each from different parts of the room.

If it's a huge crowd of thousands or more, it might be just people in the first couple of rows. But whomever I'm connecting with, I try to make it a *real*, human connection, not just a superficial stare.

Some trainers of public speaking recommend "spraying the room" with your gaze, that is, trying to meet as many people's eyes as quickly as possible, even if only for fraction of a second. I think this is a total mistake. It is much better to connect with fewer people, but really connect. I try to connect not just with the eyes, but with the heart.

––––––––––

Darren LaCroix is a 2001 World Champion of Public Speaking who now travels the globe in his own successful speaking career (www.DarrenLaCroix.com). He also regards eye contact as crucial to his craft.

LACROIX: I was filming myself giving practice speeches, and analyzing the videos. By the way, this is something few people take the time to do when preparing for a speech, but everyone should if they're serious about it. Well, I noticed that the overhead lights were reflecting off my glasses in such a way that you couldn't see my eyes through the glare. You know what I did? I went out and bought a $300 pair of ultra-thin, anti-glare eyeglasses. This was when I had no money, before I was a successful professional speaker. That was a lot of money for me then. But I bought them anyway. *That's* how important I think it is for the audience to connect with my eyes. Eye contact allows the audience to see me in my own authenticity.

ELLSBERG: But what if you're up there, being paid to motivate people and elevate them, and for whatever reason you're in a down or depressed mood. Wouldn't authenticity work against you?

LACROIX: There are two sides to this. Of course, public speaking is a stage craft. It's a form of theater. I have to leave my troubles at the door—they'll be there when I'm back [laughing].

On the other hand, I should emphasize that I don't get paid

to motivate or elevate people. I get paid to change their perspective. I'm most likely to do that when I'm being authentic with them.

I remember one talk I gave; I had a horrible flu. I was feverish, could barely stand up. But instead of pretending everything was OK, I got up there, looked at the audience straight, and said, "I'm battling an intense flu right now. I'm going to give this talk everything I've got, but I just want you to know what's going on for me." Then I didn't say another word about it, and I gave the best talk I possibly could have.

Afterwards, people came up to me and said that one authentic comment was one of the most powerful aspects of the speech, and thanked me for it. People are craving authenticity.

———

The other way communication flows is from the audience to the speaker. 1990 World Champion David Brooks (no, not the *New York Times* columnist, he pointed out to me on the phone with a chuckle) emphasized this when I spoke with him. Brooks also enjoys a successful career as a public speaker (www.davidbrooks texas.com) as well as a coach to other speakers. Brooks is passionate about the importance of reading your audience's reactions and adjusting your talk according to the cues you receive.

BROOKS: My students commonly fear eye contact because they don't want to know how the audience is reacting to them. Well, how are you going to know if you're doing a good job or not if you don't know how they're reacting to you?

Some teachers of public speaking say you should pick a spot over the audience's head and look there. Well, that's just preposterous. You should be looking audience members right in the eyes. Out of the whole body, the best reactions are in the eyes and the eyebrows. A *huge* amount of emotion is conveyed in the movement of the eyebrows alone.

———

Both Brooks and LaCroix hold an interesting perspective on the issue of singling out friendly versus unfriendly faces in the audience for special visual attention.

BROOKS: An incredibly common mistake amateurs make is to focus too much on hostile faces.

I was giving a full-day seminar in Little Rock, Arkansas. By the end of the first fifteen minutes, the audience was all with me—except for one woman, dead center in the second row. She had the nastiest glare, and it wouldn't stop. Her arms were crossed; her brows were furrowed. I was thinking, "Is my zipper down? Is there something stuck at the end of my shoe?"

Well, I committed that amateur mistake. Whenever I looked away from her, soon I would find my eyes drawing back to hers. I wanted to see if I had won her over yet, if she was still mad at me. Soon, thoughts about her and why she hated my talk were consuming almost all my mental energy up there. It started tripping me up—I was obsessing about it.

After the seminar, after most people had left, she started walking toward me. I thought, "Uh oh, I'm about to really hear it now." She said, "I just wanted to thank you. That was the best seminar I've ever attended. It changed my life." I thought, "Well, why didn't you tell your face that!" You wouldn't believe how common stories like this are among professional speakers. Don't allow negative faces to trip you up. Some people are just intense learners, and they furrow their brows while they learn.

What does Brooks recommend instead? Don't single out the hostile or the friendly faces for special attention. Make eye contact with everyone—*except* in one circumstance: if you are tripping up. Then, connect and reconnect as much as possible with the friendly faces in the crowd.

BROOKS: You can seek and find comfort in friendly faces. It's like when you were a little kid, and you really screwed up, and you went home to Mom, and she gave you that look that only a mother can give, that look that says, "It's OK. You can stumble, trip, and fall as much as you will, and it will all be OK." You can find that in a few friendly faces in almost any crowd, even if you are screwing up—in fact, especially if you are screwing up. There will always be someone there who is sympathetic to you. Focus on them in that case, and it will get you back on your feet and past the idea that the audience is against you.

LaCroix concurs with the advice to avoid our tendency to focus on negative faces in the crowd.

LACROIX: This is so common. We see the one person who's right up front, the one who's not laughing, and we want to "get" them. We want to win them over to our side. Well, what happens instead is that person brings you down. Instead, I recommend that you always come back to the happy, supportive faces. They feed us as speakers, and that allows us to feed everyone in the room.

ELLSBERG: How long should you look at one person?

LACROIX: Three to five heartbeats. Not seconds, heartbeats. Connection with the audience is something you *feel* in your body; it's not something you count.

Relational Presence

Of all the sources out there in the vast literature on public speaking, one of the experts I've found with the highest degree of subtlety in his understanding and use of eye contact is Lee

Glickstein, author of *Be Heard Now!: Tap into Your Inner Speaker and Communicate with Ease.*

I watched a video of Glickstein addressing a room, and he is like no other speaker I've seen. I found myself hanging off his every word, even when what he was saying was quite normal.

Why? Glickstein practices and teaches something he calls "relational presence" in public speaking, which he told me is "the capacity to be with one person at a time in full accessibility, even if you're talking to a large audience." Whatever he is saying, he is always saying it *to somebody* in the group, not to the group as a whole—delivering it right into that person's eyes.

Glickstein (www.speakingcircles.com) told me he came up with this style of public speaking out of fear. He was so terrified of large groups when he got his start in public speaking that he had to break the group down into smaller units—namely, the individuals that constituted the group—so as not to be overwhelmed. "I thought this was just coping. It turned out this is what the masterful communicators do already. They may not even be able to explain what they're doing."

All teachers of public speaking recognize the importance of eye contact in establishing a connection. However, many teachers make an error of extrapolation: Because eye contact is important, you should strive to make eye contact with as *many* audience members as possible, even if you only connect with them for a second or two.

According to Glickstein, this is a big mistake. He writes in *Be Heard Now:*

> The larger the audience, the more these speakers fragment their energy. They feel pressure to scan and move, sweep and hurry—and often scurry around the stage in the process. This

approach tends to be distracting, stressful, and disconnecting, both for the speaker and for the audience!

For eye contact to have impact, it needs to be at a deeper level. . . . The ideal is to engage each person we focus on 100 percent, not to contact 100 percent of the people. At first, some speakers are afraid that by engaging individuals for that long, they will exclude the rest of the audience. Just the opposite is true. Listeners feel more fully included and connected with us when we make deeper connections, even if we make fewer of them. The group values quality of connection more than quantity of contacts, so there is no need to "cover" for everyone in the audience.[1]

Glickstein recommends that instead of scanning the audience and making one or two seconds of eye contact with many different people, the speaker make five to ten seconds of contact with any given listener before moving on. I've seen him do this on video, and the effect on the crowd is electrifying, even through the video. I sat in the edge of my seat, waiting to hear what he would say next. It is easy to pick up when a real connection is being made between two people, and that feels a lot different than when a speaker is droning on without making any connection at all.

When I spoke with Glickstein, he repeatedly emphasized the importance of *listening* while speaking to your audience. This confused me.

ELLSBERG: Isn't it the *audience* that is supposed to be listening?

GLICKSTEIN: Some people hear the word "listening," and they think, "How can you listen while you're speaking?" I use it in a different sense, of receptivity to that person's whole being. The way I think of it is cherishing the individual you're talking with. To me, that's a kind of listening.

———————

This is a subtle distinction to convey in words, but talking to Glickstein in person, I felt what he was talking about instantly. As we talked together, whether he was talking to me or I was talking to him, I felt as though his presence was completely with me—that no part of his mental bandwidth was going toward anything other than our conversation.

Think for a moment how uncommon this is in our current world of text messages, instant messaging, Facebook, Twitter, and BlackBerries. I know from my own experience that whomever I'm speaking with, often there's a dialogue going in the back of my mind that has nothing to do with the conversation—"Darn, I forgot to get that e-mail out today; I need to remember to do it tomorrow . . . Oh, I need to pick up the vegetables for tonight's dinner on the way home . . ." Sound familiar?

Yet talking with Glickstein, who has devoted a great part of his life to developing the capacity to be present in interpersonal communication, I had the refreshing experience of talking to someone who seemed to have none of that going on—he was just completely *here*.

In addition, I felt a total lack of judgment. How many of us—and I don't exclude myself here at all—can truly say that we are never judging or evaluating people when we speak to them, or in some other way seeing how that person can *fit in* to our predetermined plans or agenda? Talking to Glickstein, I felt as though he was just being with me, in a compassionate, accepting presence, without expecting anything of me or judging me. It felt wonderful.

Imagine if you could make your *entire audience* feel that way. This is what Glickstein trains his clients to do.

GLICKSTEIN: This doesn't mean you need to spend an enormous amount of time with each audience member. If you fully cherish someone in the audience you're relating to, they'll feel that, even if it is only for a few seconds before you gently move your attention to the next audience member.

Connection with your audience is not something you *do*. It is something that you *allow*. If you're *trying* to connect with your audience, you are coming from the assumption that you are currently disconnected from them. But the best speakers have the sense that they are already connected to others they're speaking with. They're just uncovering that connection.

Most public speaking trainings teach "connect, connect, with eye contact." Well, you can't connect through eye contact, or with anything else. The connection is already there. You allow the connection to reveal itself, through availability.

Eye contact is taught as a *technique*. This implies a very superficial way to think about it. "Eye contact" doesn't mean anything to me. It's being-to-being contact. Really, presence is heart-to-heart. The eyes just show whom it's directed toward.

Naturally, as someone who is writing a book on eye contact, I don't agree with this last thought completely. I do believe the eyes have a special place in the human experience for fostering connection. But I appreciate Glickstein's thoughts on this, because they point us toward an important truth about connecting with others:

If we *attempt* to connect with others with some kind of "technique," be it eye contact or anything else, the result is, at best, the simulation of connection. Instead, our connection must be whole—with our attention, our presence, and our availability for the other person. (We touched upon this difference in the section on networking in Chapter 5.)

These are subtle distinctions, but you know it when you feel it in person. You just *know* when someone is totally present and available to you, versus when they have some kind of wall or filter or other distance between you. It's a quality of being.

You've probably felt many different shades of this at cocktail parties or networking events.

How does one get better at relational presence? Glickstein recommends a practice he calls "5 and 5." This involves finding a partner. If you are speaking first, you talk for five minutes about whatever is on your mind. Or you could say nothing at all if that's where you are in the moment. The other person's job is to simply be there and listen—but really listen, not just with the eyes, but with the heart, the soul, everything. Be completely available for the other person, nonjudgmentally. Cherish the other person. Then it's your turn to do the same.

Glickstein has developed subtle ideas about what the rest of our face is doing when we make eye contact. In particular, I was struck by his recommendation that speakers practice listening to their audience, with full presence, but without the nodding up and down, "uh-huh"ing, and "yes"ing that we often do unconsciously, or that some schools of communication such as "active listening" encourage us to do.

His reason makes a lot of sense. When we're nodding and "yes"ing, we're often doing it unconsciously, out of a general desire to be genial and agreeable. It often has more to do with our own desire to be liked than with a commitment to be fully present to the other person. Still, I had some questions about this.

ELLSBERG: Isn't it a little severe to have no smile while listening?

GLICKSTEIN: Students often ask that. That's when I say, "Remember your sense of positive regard for the other person. Cherish the other person." That will shine through, whether you're smiling or not.

Then my students say, "Yeah, but I'd like to smile!" And I

say, "Well, it depends. Is your smile coming from just a natural glow, or is it coming from that reactive, habitual, validating impulse?" There's so much of that desire to be validated that's unconscious. I like my students to try going the other way, just to feel what it's like.

I had a student who had been a top-level executive assistant all her life. At one point, she said, "I watched the video of me speaking, and I noticed I was smiling all the time. I can't stop smiling, I just can't stop. And it feels wrong. I want to not smile so much."

At one point, as she was talking about this in front of our practice group, the smile disappeared from her face suddenly, and she looked as if she was boiling inside. "I'm so in touch right now with the rage I feel for having to smile all day long at my bosses. I hate it—I want to not have to smile so much." She got in touch with how she was giving her power away with her false smile.

We have no idea what is inside of us, authentically, until we quit with the habitual and programmed smiles. This is a big issue, particularly for a lot of women in our society, who are under a lot of pressure to be pleasant and congenial all the time.

There's nothing wrong with a smile as a glow. This kind of smile comes from the inside—it's not plastered onto the outside of the face. Ultimately, when it comes to a smile, only you know if you're covering something else up with it.

PowerPoints, Prepared Papers, Big Rooms, and Other Challenges

Under the mantra of "multimedia," most presentations these days include PowerPoint or other audiovisual presentations.

Yet have you ever noticed how frequent these presentations act like a visually administered sleeping pill? When someone pulls out the projector or a laptop to start a PowerPoint presentation, a reflexive urge arises in me to pull out my earplugs and eye mask for a little snooze.

Why is it that visual presentations are often so sleep inducing? I asked Diane DiResta, author of *Knockout Presentations: How to Deliver Your Message with Power, Punch, and Pizzazz*, for her thoughts on this topic. DiResta (www.diresta.com) is a communications coach whose client list includes AT&T, Chase, IBM, Reuters, IBM, and the NBA. She has been cited in the *Wall Street Journal* and the *New York Times*.

DIRESTA: The biggest mistake people make when using PowerPoint and other visual presentations is that they read the slides. That transforms you from an expert in your subject matter, offering your expertise to your audience, into a mere reader of notes.

Everything we've been learning up until this point suggests that audiences respond most to your *sense of presence and connection* to the audience. I believe this is even more important than the subject matter. In college, I had a sociology professor who could turn the most mundane subject matter—regression analysis in statistics, for example—into an exciting presentation that had us on the edge of our seats, merely by his ability to connect with each of us individually, his care that we *got* the material, and his enthusiastic presence.

In turn, I had numerous professors who managed to turn some of the most potentially gripping material—wars, revolutions, lively philosophical debates throughout history, great poets—into verbal sleeping pills, largely because their noses were buried in their notes.

To counteract this latter pitfall, DiResta advocates a system she calls "Touch, Turn, and Talk."

DIRESTA: The first step is to "touch" the first bullet of your slide with your visual field and gestures, so that your audience knows that you are referring to that slide. Next, turn and face your audience. Now talk to them about the content of the slides while making direct eye contact with individual members. End your words on a pair of eyes. Then turn back, and "touch" the next bullet visually, and the round starts over again. Turn back to your audience, and speak on that point. *There is no reason for you to look at your slides while you are speaking about them.* If you need a refresher on the material of each slide, come prepared with an outline and bullet points in front of you. But looking back transforms you from an expert into a reader and makes the audience's faith and interest in you plunge.

When it's time to change slides, you can turn back to the slide once there's a new one. But always end your last words on a pair of eyes before you turn back to the slide. This keeps your audience connected as you turn away from them.

———

Another mistake DiResta sees frequently among public speakers and presenters is burying your head in your prepared speech or notes, rather than talking to the audience.

DIRESTA: Prepared manuscripts are the hardest kind of speech to make interesting. In fact, I recommend against delivering prewritten speeches if at all possible. Of course, that's not always feasible. If you're delivering a report that is going to be dissected, parsed, and analyzed by the media, then you're going to have to work from a preplanned statement. But in any other circumstance, I would recommend against it.

———

Why? Because, unless you have a teleprompter, it's so darn hard not to just bury your nose in the manuscript. Again, you become a reader—something almost anyone in the room could do—rather than expert talking to an audience. DiResta recommends giving a talk from a basic sketch outline of notes or pictograms (drawn representations of your ideas). Better yet (and this is for more advanced speakers): Memorize the outline so you don't have any prepared material in front of you at all.

If you must give a talk from a manuscript—for example, if you are representing a company in your talk and the legal department has to vet your every word—DiResta recommends doing a *lot* of work marking up the manuscript so that it is as readable as possible, giving you the maximum chance to take moments to connect with your audience visually. She recommends using large type (at least 14 to 16 point), breaking it up into outline form with headings and subheadings, and perhaps even breaking up individual ideas into bullet points. Underline key points / and break up your ideas with slashes like this / to indicate where you can pause and look up at your audience.

Look at your first phrase or sentence. Then look up at the audience and deliver it to one person, being sure to end the phrase or sentence while still making eye contact. Then look down and read your next phrase or sentence. Then look back up again. This is analogous to the "Touch, Turn, and Talk" system she recommends for using visual aids.

Still, the ideal situation by far is not to require *any* supporting material in front of you. This is what the real pros do—the ones who know how to whip a room into a frenzy. You reach this level when you know material cold, not just as a memorized speech. You've internalized the concepts so deeply that you can talk extemporaneously on them, creating the speech as you talk. This allows you to own the stage, walking to different sides to connect with different parts of the room. It allows you to use big hand gestures. Most importantly, it allows you to focus nearly all of your energy on *connecting with your audience personally*, which is why they came to see you live in the first place.

SEVEN

If Looks Could Kill

Eye Contact in Hostile, Aggressive, or Competitive Situations

Two people who stare each other in the eye for sixty seconds straight will soon either be fighting or making love.[1]
—ATTRIBUTED TO PIERCE BUTLER

Thou tell'st me there is murder in mine eye. . . .
—SHAKESPEARE, *As You Like It*[2]

The California Kid," also known as Urijah Faber, is a compact man, about five-six and a hundred and forty-five pounds. He's the kind of guy many taller, larger guys would probably think they could take down easily in a bar brawl.

But those taller, larger men would be wrong. Urijah Faber could have nearly any man on the ground within a few seconds, gasping for last breaths, if given reason or provocation.

Faber is a world champion of mixed martial arts (MMA), the highly technical yet brutal formerly underground sport that exploded into international pop culture after the reality show *The Ultimate Fighter* hit cable TV in 2005. In this sport, closer to no-holds-barred fighting than traditional martial arts competitions, fighters trained in various styles, including boxing, kickboxing, wrestling, jiujitsu, and judo, square off to see who is the best overall fighter in a free-form event with minimal rules or formalities. The fights can be bloody and can push fighters to the limits of physical and psychological endurance.

However, within this sport, Faber—who has held title belts in the World Extreme Cagefighting, King of the Cage, and Gladiator Challenge leagues—is known as a good-spirited, positive, friendly guy, not an arrogant or cocky trash-talker. The latter is an image some others in the sport cultivate deliberately, in contrast to Faber.

I met up with Faber (www.urijahfaber.com) in his hometown of Sacramento, California. Until now, in this book, we've been talking about the ways eye contact is used to create connection and rapport. Now, we turn our attention to explore the role of eye contact in a very different context: intimidation and even self-defense in competitive, hostile, or dangerous situations.

During our time together, text messages from Faber's many female admirers streamed in a few per minute, all expressing hopes for spending the evening with him—but I was flattered that during our interview, he ignored these beckons and gave me his undivided attention.

ELLSBERG: How do you use eye contact when you fight?

FABER: I feel the calmer you are with your eye contact, the more intimidating it is. It's obvious that you're focused and you're not being friendly in your eyes, but it's more of a confidence in your eyes that sends the message that you mean business. I think that's more intimidating than a real aggressive stare.

A lot of these guys that are overdoing it are insecure themselves. Some guys might have some sort of crazy look that they give to psych someone out. But for the most part, if you watch the best guys, most of them just look eager and confident.

I would say that in a real situation—in a bar or fight situation, that kind of calm confidence will carry its weight over an intimidating look that's supposed to look scary. Being a smaller guy, I've been in situations where I've been approached by guys that for whatever reason are trying to make themselves feel good or to impress someone else, or have something to prove.

As soon as they come on aggressive, and they see your reaction as zero fear and zero intimidation and zero backing down, that's usually the most intimidating thing, and it nips things in the bud. It's through eye contact, not only the expression in your eyes, but your ability to focus on the person—whether you're looking away or straight at him, whether you're having any kind of change in emotion—it can all be seen in the eyes. Someone who's not scared, you can tell by looking in the eyes.

In an MMA title fight, you'll see fighters looking for signs of fear in each other's eyes in the "staredowns" before the fights. In MMA, the "staredown" is a tried-and-true crowd-pleaser, where the two fighters stand face to face, inches apart, and attempt to psych each other via focused gaze before the fight.

These staredowns are popular with fans because they're so intense. Accordingly, many of them are posted on YouTube. com. Some staredowns involve a lot of trash-talking (look up "Rampage Jackson vs. Rashad Evans staredown" on YouTube for a particularly juicy example), but perhaps the most chilling ones are pure, cold white flame (search for "Don Frye vs. Ken Shamrock—Pride FC 19 Bad Blood").

The difference between these two styles of eye intimidation can be seen in a 2005 staredown before a match between Faber, known for his cool, collected demeanor, and Charles "Krazy Horse" Bennett, known for his trash-talking during the fights and his fast lifestyle outside of the ring. (Look up "Urijah Faber vs. Charles Bennett" on YouTube.) Bennett leans forward and sniffs both of Faber's armpits one after the other in a mocking gesture, while Faber remains unfazed, maintaining his cool, collected stare right back. Four and a half minutes into the fight, Bennett is lying prone, face pushed into the mat as Faber is strangling him from on top, and the match is over.

Staring at Lions

The staredowns aren't just limited to humans about to fight. In an amazing clip I found on YouTube called "Lion vs. Human Staredown," a man named Mike Penman, a gamekeeper in Botswana, gets out of a safari truck near two lions under a tree and begins crawling on all fours toward the lions. "There's no written recipe on how to approach lions on all fours," he says, deadpan, as he gets out of the truck. Soon he is closer to the lions than to the truck, ensuring that if he provokes them too much, he will have no escape.

One lion growls, gets up on his own fours, and begins walking toward Penman with a determined stare. It's amazing how much this stare resembles a human stare of aggression. "If you get too close, I'm going to seriously *$%# you up," the lion's gaze says, loud and clear. While you can't see Penman's gaze, as his back is to the camera, it's obvious that the stare between the two beings is intense. At a few points, the lion appears to begin a charge, but Penman backs him off with a "stop" gesture. The language of bodies apparently knows no species boundaries.

Whether among humans or animals, nature has endowed us with few resources more powerful for forcing others to back off, back down, and step away than a direct, focused, unwavering gaze. This is a key component of the posture of resolve and determination Darwin discusses at length in *The Expression of the Emotions in Man and Animals*. It says, loud and clear, "I'm here, ready for action, and I will not back down." Or, in other words, "Over my dead body."

When in a situation where this kind of defense is necessary (please don't try this against lions, though!) the key is not to take your gaze away from your opponent's eyes until the interaction is over. It will throw your opponent off, and they will need to muster an enormous amount of mental and emotional energy to get themselves back into emotional composure and meet your gaze again, at which point they'll be knocked back off balance by the unflagging laser beams coming out of your eyes.

The intent of the gaze here is completely different than in the situations we've been talking about in the rest of the book. Everything in this book, up until this point, has been about making, deepening, and maintaining connections with other people. In the examples in this chapter, however, the point is not to create and maintain a connection but rather to *break* a connection: to get the other person to back off or submit to you, without any harm to your own body or ego.

Thus, the quality of the gaze is also completely different. Rather than warm, inviting pools with a soft, forgiving focus, our eyes become tightly focused, ready to penetrate the opponent with resolve.

In *On Seeing: Things Seen, Unseen, and Obscene*, F. González-

Crussi discusses at length "the deeply rooted belief that some persons can harm others by merely looking at them: the so-called 'evil eye,' of which tales and folklore exist in practically all cultures." González-Crussi points out that "early theories on the mechanism of vision proposed that a stream of invisible particles flowed out of the ocular globe toward the object viewed. This being the case, the particles ejected could be hurtful to others."[3]

Clearly, the power of a gaze to cut down, intimidate, or frighten another was not lost on our ancestors. More recently in history, Ralph Waldo Emerson writes: "An eye can threaten like a loaded and levelled gun, or can insult like hissing or kicking."[4]

A lot of this effect, to be sure, has to do with facial expressions. Whether you adopt the trash-talking posturing of some MMA fighters or the cool, collected confidence of Urijah Faber when using eyes and expression for aggressive purposes, your face does not convey the openhearted acceptance and intimacy that would be appropriate in a dating situation, or the respectful openness in a business situation, but rather intense resolve to defend or impose your will in the situation.

"This Is MY Locker Room"

Nick Bollettieri is one of the most legendary tennis coaches in the history of the game. He has coached nine tennis players ranked number one in the world: Andre Agassi, Boris Becker, Jim Courier, Martina Hingis, Marcelo Rios, Monica Seles, Venus Williams, Serena Williams, and Maria Sharapova. He is the founder of IMG Academies in Florida, one of the most elite sports training schools in the world (www.imgacademies .com).

ELLSBERG: Do you think eye contact is an important factor in competitive sports?

BOLLETTIERI: Let me answer with an anecdote. At Wimbledon, there are two locker rooms. One of them, called "Uptown," is only for quarterfinalists and above, and past champions. When Boris Becker walked into that room with his beanie cap and his bags over his shoulder, the first thing he'd do is have a good, long look at each man in the room, straight in the eyes. He didn't say a word, but his eyes said everything: "This is *my* locker room. What the hell are *you* doing in *my* locker room?" Right then and there, his match began, by his look.

When you're playing tennis, football, basketball—when you look into the other guy's eyes, they can tell whether you're peeing in your pants or whether you're ready to continue battle. When Michael Jordan shot three-pointers, if you just looked at his eyes and his body motions, without looking at the basket, you wouldn't know whether he made it or missed it. In his eyes—and in everything he had—he made that shot. That gives a loud message to the audience *and to the opposition.*

You could be up 5–0 against Becker, and he'd still be looking at you: "You don't have me beat yet. This battle isn't over." If you go walk past the net and your head is down, and you've got your shoulders slumped, and fear in your eyes, what are you saying? You've given the message that it's over.

Matt Furey and the "Thousand-Mile Stare"

Matt Furey is the author of *Combat Conditioning: Functional Exercises for Fitness and Combat Sports* and one of the most respected trainers of "functional fitness" conditioning for martial artists in the world (strength training using body weight and naturalistic movements rather than weights). A national champion wrestler in college, Furey later trained in the ancient Chinese martial art Shuai-Chiao, a form of kung fu. In 1997, Furey became the first non-Chinese to win the world championship of Shuai-Chiao, in Beijing. He is the author of a very popular online fitness newsletter (www.mattfurey.com).

I asked Furey what he saw as the role of eye contact in prevailing in hostile or aggressive situations.

FUREY: There's no question that eye contact plays a big role in intimidation. Anything you can do to break the confidence of the other guy will be invaluable in a competitive or aggressive situation. With eye contact, this can happen even before the battle begins. From warfare in the time of the Greeks and Romans, to sporting battles today, history is full of examples where, as soon as the other guy sees the look of resolve and determination in your eyes, he knows he's lost the fight before it's even begun.

ELLSBERG: What are some specific techniques to project this sense of dominance and intimidation through your eyes?

FUREY: There's something called the "thousand-mile stare." The name says it all. You look the guy right in the eyes, but like he's not even there. You're looking right through him, at a point a thousand miles off in the distance. This reduces the guy to nothing. It says, "You're not relevant. You're not even there. I'm going to walk right through you. You're as meaningless as a patch of air in front of me."

Furey told me an amazing story of his use of eye contact in a competitive situation. In some ways it flies in the face of everything we've been discussing, as it is an example of how to use connecting (rather than domineering) eye contact in a hostile situation. But in another sense, it is the exception that proves the rule.

FUREY: When I was a wrestler for the University of Iowa, we'd often be at competitions with the team from the University of Oklahoma. Well, there was a guy on the Oklahoma team named Dave Schultz, who went on to win a gold medal in wrestling at the 1984 Olympics.

I never wrestled Shultz, but a lot of my teammates did, and I got to observe him a lot. And he did something that drove my teammates crazy. Before each match he'd come up to his Iowa opponent—look him right in the eyes, shake hands and say, "Hey, what's going on? How's everything going? How are you doing?" He'd be slapping other Iowa guys' backs, laughing and having a good time. Then before he left, he'd look his opponent right in the eyes again and say, "Good luck."

This just drove the guys on my team nuts. "Who is that guy, coming over here and being all buddy-buddy with us? Who does he think he is?" And then Shultz would win his match with the Iowa guy later on. I feel his actions gave him a psychological edge.

What was he doing with that strategy? He was demonstrating absolute fearlessness. He was so confident. He could appear completely casual, social, and friendly with his opponents, like he owned the place. We were the guests at his party, and he was the host. We were on his turf. And of course, when you tell your opponent "good luck," what does that imply? That he needs it.

I used this technique that I learned from Dave when I was at the world championship in Shuai-Chiao. Right before the championship match, my opponent was at the edge of the mat, getting mentally ready. I walked right over to him, stuck out my hand to shake his, looked him right in the eyes, and with a friendly smile, said "Good luck." He weakly shook my hand and nodded at me, but the look that washed over this guy's face was priceless. It was this mix of shock, horror, contempt, anger, and fear. It was obvious no one had ever done this to him before. It threw him completely off balance. The match was tough, but I won, and if doing that before the match gave me even a one-percent edge, that was the percent I needed to win the championship title.

EIGHT

Truth and Eyes

Eye Contact and Lie Detection

*The balls of sight are so formed, that one man's eyes are
spectacles to another, to read his heart with.*

—SAMUEL JOHNSON[1]

Giovanni Vigliotto was a short, squat man who worked
as a flea market merchant during the seventies and early
eighties. One might infer, from this résumé, that he was not a
world-class seducer of women.

Yet, Vigliotto had a gallant way about him. "He was always
touchingly concerned about [women's] welfare, a perfect gen-
tleman to the point of being courtly, and endearingly self-
pitying," a news piece said.[2] "I never realized there was any
other way to treat a woman than the way I do. Is it wrong for a
man to hold the door for a woman to pass through? Is it wrong
to buy them flowers?" he once told a reporter.[3]

His chivalrous nature recalled an earlier and more famous

ladies' man by the same first name, Don Giovanni; and for many women, his charms turned out to be equally irresistible. So much so, in fact, that in 1981 a Mesa, Arizona, real estate broker named Patricia Gardiner accepted a proposal and married him only eight days after meeting him at a swap meet.

A few years later, in a Phoenix courtroom, however, she discovered that she was not his first—or even his *only*—wife. There were, he said, 104 others he had married in a row—*and he had yet to divorce any of them.* (This later earned him a spot in the *Guinness Book of World Records* as the man with the most bigamous marriages in history.)

Weeks after they were married, he persuaded Gardiner to sell her home, which she did promptly. The plan was that they would drive separately to California to begin a new life together, he in a van with all her possessions and $36,000 of her cash. When she arrived in San Diego, she waited for him in their honeymoon hotel, as they had arranged. And waited. And waited.

He had told her he had "$49 million in savings and owned the *Queen Mary* ocean liner docked in Long Beach, Calif."[4] Now she was penniless in the hotel, with no worldly possessions, and with no shoulder to cry on other than that of her poodle.

What allowed her to get swept away in such a disastrous romantic fantasy? "He looked right into my face and eyes. I liked that honest trait," Gardiner told *Time* magazine.[5]

Surely it would be fair to dismiss Gardiner as a nincompoop who deserved her fate. It would make sense to read this as a story about one woman's gullibility, not a story about how easy it is to deceive and be deceived.

But here's the thing. Vigliotto (who used that moniker to sound more romantic than his birth name, Fred Jipp) seduced *dozens* of other women into such tragic charades. To some women, he was a rich retiree; to others, a mafia don. Anything that made it sound like they had just walked into the plot of their favorite romance novel.

Six months before Gardiner and Vigliotto met, newlywed Sharon Clark was pacing in an Ontario motel, barefoot, abandoned by Vigliotto on their honeymoon, and out $49,000 in cash and valuables lent to Vigliotto *three weeks after she had met him.* A few months before that, Joan Bacarella was waiting in a motel room for Vigliotto to return, after she had divorced her husband, married Vigliotto (he had proposed within a day of meeting her), and lent Vigliotto $1,600 cash and $40,000 of inventory from her small business—shortly after they met.

It is not only "bored, middle-aged, and provincial" women seeking romantic escapism, as one account portrayed Vigliotto's victims,[6] who fall prey to bald-faced but comforting lies promulgated by a confident, charming, and "honest seeming" character face to face. We all do. In fact, even people whose very job description is (or should be) skepticism and critical inquiry do as well. Here is a passage from my father Daniel Ellsberg's book *Secrets: A Memoir of Vietnam and the Pentagon Papers,* describing the press corps' relation to my father's boss in the Pentagon, Assistant Secretary of Defense John McNaughton:

> *I often watched McNaughton with reporters, because he called me into his office whenever he had to give an interview. . . . I watched and marveled. John was great at this. As he got into areas where he had to be especially untruthful or elusive, his Pekin, Illinois, accent got broader till he sounded like someone discussing corn at a country fair or standing on the rail of a riverboat. [Note: he had previously worked as a full professor of law at the Harvard Law School.] You looked for hayseed in his*

cuffs. He simply didn't mind looking and sounding like a hick in the interests of dissimulation . . . [I]t was very effective. Reporters would tell me how "open" my boss was, compared with others they ran into, this after I had listened to an hour of whoppers. It became clear to me that journalists had no idea, no clue, just how often and egregiously they were lied to.[7]

It is simply not the case, as the Eagles sing, that "you can't hide your lyin' eyes."

But wait—doesn't this go against the entire message of this book? Haven't I spent chapters discussing how the eyes and eye contact give us instant, intuitive, reliable information about a person's interior emotional state?

Yes. But emotions and thoughts are very different phenomena. In most cases the word "lie" refers to thoughts: making a claim one knows to be false, with the intention to deceive. To understand why body language does not betray thoughts as readily as it betrays emotions, we must recognize a key difference between emotions and thoughts.

Body language in general and eye contact in particular give us a very good read on a person's emotions. They are, to use a term common in evolutionary theory, "signals" of a person's emotions, meaning that one thing (wide eyes, for example) is so frequently conjoined with another (fear or surprise) that one can be taken as reliable evidence of the other.

However, Paul Ekman—widely regarded as the world's greatest expert on facial expressions and deception—goes to great pains to remind us that thoughts (unlike emotions) give off no signal whatsoever. They pass without the slightest trace on our body, in and of themselves.

[M]ost emotions have a signal. That is, they let others know what is happening inside us, unlike thoughts, for which there

is not a distinctive signal for the various thoughts people have. . . . When people find out I study facial expression, they often get very uncomfortable, saying, "You are reading my mind." I say, "No, I can only read your emotions." I cannot tell from the signal what caused the emotion. If I see a fear expression, I know that you perceive a threat. But the fear of being disbelieved looks just like the fear of being caught. Recognizing that is important in police work. If a suspect is afraid, that does not tell you that he or she committed the crime. Maybe, but maybe not. That was Othello's error. He thought his wife Desdemona's look of fear was the fear of a woman caught in infidelity. But it was a wife's fear of her jealous husband, who had just killed someone he thought was her lover: She should have been afraid. [8]

Unless a person is incredibly wound up inside by lying, or otherwise terrified of getting caught, lies per se do not show up in an easily detectable way in someone's body language or eyes. For most of us, by the time our arm has grown long enough to reach the proverbial cookie jar, we have also grown comfortable with lying in some circumstances. Which means that when we do lie, our bodies won't show telltale signs of nervousness—at least not enough to be easily detected.

A telling example of this dynamic is the well-known phenomenon that psycopaths often make extremely solid, piercing eye contact. Upon his first meeting with a psychopath in a prison, psychopathy expert Robert Hare writes, "the eye contact he made with me was so direct and intense that I wondered if I had ever really looked anybody in the eye before. That stare was unrelenting—he didn't indulge in the brief glances away that most people use to soften the force of their gaze."[9] Psychopaths, almost by definition, are people with no emotional discomfort at breaking moral taboos, which perhaps contributes to the ease with which they can lie—and much worse—without betraying the slightest signs of discomfort in their eyes or bodies because there is none to betray.

Short of such extreme examples, for the rest of us, any emotional discomfort we have at lying can usually be suppressed, stuffed, or otherwise concealed to the point where others cannot detect the lie.

We opened the book with Bill Clinton and his legendary power of rapport and connection through eye contact. Well, he also had another less noble way with his eyes—an easy way with lying, when he looked into the eyes of reporters at a 1998 White House press conference and said, calmly and confidently:

> I want to say one thing to the American people. I want you to listen to me. I'm going to say this again: I did not have sexual relations with that woman, Miss Lewinsky. I never told anybody to lie, not a single time; never. These allegations are false, and I need to go back to work for the American people.

Of course, not everyone believed him when he said it, but millions did. They felt shock, surprise, and even personal betrayal later that year when their president looked directly into the camera and into their eyes via national television and said in a solemn tone: "Indeed I did have a relation with Miss Lewinsky that was not appropriate."

Ekman has performed dozens of experiments over decades, summarized in a paper entitled "Why Don't We Catch Liars?" which test empirically how good we are at spotting lies from demeanor alone. Typically, members of one subject group are given a monetary incentive to lie convincingly about something, as well as a (lesser) incentive to tell the truth convincingly. They get to choose whether they lie during an experimental interrogation. Members of another subject group watch videotapes of these interrogations and are asked to determine whether the person is lying or not.

In another scenario, aspiring nursing students were told they were being evaluated—as part of school entrance requirements—for their ability to conceal their emotions in stressful circumstances that they were told was a necessary part of efficient hospital work. They were asked to watch videos either of tranquil ocean scenes or of gruesome medical operations and footage of burn victims. The ones who had seen the gruesome footage were instructed to try to convince an interviewer (being tested for lie-detection ability) that they had actually been watching a film about meadow flowers.

Ekman and his colleagues have found, consistently over decades through experiments like these, that most people's determination of others' lying were generally no better than flipping a coin. This held true even when those attempting to detect the lies were "customs officials, policemen, trial court judges, FBI, CIA, BATF, DEA, forensic psychiatrists, and trial lawyers."[10]

However, there is a caveat. What we have been discussing so far is people's *untrained* ability to detect lies from demeanor. Ekman has exhaustively catalogued what he calls "micro expressions," split-second facial expressions of emotion that are difficult to detect unless you know what to look for. He has developed an interactive module called the Micro Expression Training Tool (www.paulekman.com) to help detect these expressions. He has evidence that people can get up to 75 percent accuracy in detecting lies with even a few hours of training.

Seventy-five percent accuracy is not something we'd want to base a legal system on; this kind of evidence should never be allowed in a court, just as polygraph evidence is not. But still, if you are interested in becoming more adept at detecting lies, it is possible to train in this skill, and Ekman consults with law enforcement and intelligence agencies for democratic nations around the world.

Where does this leave us on the relation between eye contact and lying? From all I have gathered on the topic, the following rules of thumb seem reliable: Eyes and body language tell us *nothing* of someone's thoughts. They can speak *volumes* about a person's emotional state—*if* that person is not consciously attempting to hide their emotional state.

When people are indeed trying to hide and/or lie about their emotional state from us, however, the evidence suggests that we humans are not nearly as good as we think we are at detecting deception—at least, not without practice. However, lying does leave telltale clues, and our capacity to detect these can be honed, augmented, and practiced to the point where we become quite effective at telling when people are lying.

I have a severe allergy to pine nuts. If I eat one, I go into a condition called anaphylaxis, which is an extreme form of swelling, such that my trachea will swell shut and prevent me from breathing within hours if I do not receive medical attention.

Needless to say, I am very careful to ask waiters if anything I've ordered has pine nuts.

Once I was in a restaurant in Manhattan, and I went through my usual spiel to the waitress. "Does the quesadilla have pine nuts in it? I have a severe allergy, and if I eat a pine nut, I go to the hospital."

The waitress said no. I asked if she could double-check, and she said she would.

When the quesadilla arrived, it came with a guacamole, but also with a green sauce that looked suspiciously like pesto, which contains pine nuts.

Before eating, I called the waitress over again and asked if she was *certain* that this wasn't pesto—if it was, I explained again, I'd be in the emergency room very shortly. "No, it's not pesto," she said.

"I'm sorry to trouble you, but could you just go and double-check again? It really does look like pesto."

She sighed and ran off to the kitchen. A few moments later, she came back and said, "I asked the chef, and he said it's spinach."

Some voice in me felt that something was still off. "Don't eat it," I heard welling up from my gut.

Still, I had now asked her four times about the pine nuts and had informed her twice about the severity of my condition. If I was going to eat in restaurants at all, another part of my mind reasoned, it seemed this was the extreme of how far I could reasonably go to double-check. I overrode that intuitive voice and bit in.

Within seconds, I could feel the allergic reaction coming on. I barged through the kitchen and found the chef. "Does the quesadilla have pesto sauce?" I asked him.

"Yeah, it's right in there with the guacamole."

The waitress had lied through her teeth.

I spent the night in the emergency room.

This story is interesting from two angles. One, I was taken in by the woman's lie. Why she lied to me about checking with the chef, I don't know, but I fell for it. (By the way, I ended up getting a modest cash settlement from the restaurant, covering the hospital bill plus enough for me to take a week of vacation that summer, so there was at least justice.)

But another interesting thing is that some part of me did know this woman was lying. It welled up from my gut as a definite feeling, however faint, that I shouldn't bite in. I chose to override that feeling, but it was absolutely there.

Jena calls this feeling the "animal instinct." She is a weight-loss coach, and she uses this concept to guide her clients into listening to what their bodies authentically crave rather than what they habitually eat out of convenience or mindless face-stuffing.

Living with Jena, I have begun to pay a lot more attention to my "animal instinct," not just around food but in all areas of my life. I find that whenever I'm facing some kind of uncertainty, usually if I listen closely enough, my body is giving me a strong answer, and usually it's a good one. This, I believe, is the capacity Ekman can train people to develop so that they become better lie catchers.

Had I paid more attention to my animal instinct, I would have listened to that voice inside of me, which was probably picking up on something in that waitress's body language.

Whenever we evaluate a situation, whether we should trust someone or not, whether we should believe someone, whether we should do business with someone, I now believe our body gives us a strong answer—in fact, screamingly strong—if we practice paying attention.

I close this chapter with one of the most eloquent and accurate examples I have come across in literature of how we intuit the inner worlds of others—beyond what their mouths say—through our instinctual reading of body language and eyes. The scene is from George Eliot's *The Mill on the Floss*. It will take a moment to set up the background of the scene, but I think it is worth your while, as it is a gorgeous description of what we've been discussing in this chapter.

Maggie Tulliver is living a socially isolated life in a run-down family home in the country. To help bring her out, her cousin Lucy Deane invites her to live with her closer to town. Maggie becomes infatuated with her cousin's suitor, the dashing Stephen Guest—and the attraction becomes mutual as the two enjoy long conversations.

Sensing this growing threat to her own love, Lucy arranges to send Maggie off on a rowing trip with an old flame of Maggie's, Philip Wakem, in hopes that their passion will rekindle. But, at the last minute, Philip becomes ill, and Maggie needs a replacement for her outing. Stephen steps forward to volunteer.

As they row, alone together at last after a budding infatuation, their passion reaches a boiling point. In what seems to be a calculated move, Stephen allows the boat to drift hours past the normal exit point on the river, and they become lost. In their flurry of worry over how to resolve the situation, Stephen proposes to her—and suggests they catch a passing boat to the next town and run off together.

Maggie never says "yes" with words, exactly, but while talking after his proposal, she begins more and more to say "yes" with her body language. He flags down a passing boat for them to carry out the plan, and she goes along with it.

Stephen manages to convince a passing ship to take them to the nearest town overnight, where they will run off and begin their new life together. They fall asleep with visions of eternal love.

The next morning, however, the winds have shifted—for Maggie, at least. She was haunted by dreams that Lucy and Philip were searching for her, and becomes wracked by guilt at the decision she has made, or at least the decision she has acquiesced to passively. In her mind, she becomes more and more determined not to carry out the plan. Stephen comes to hold her hand, thrilled that they are about to reach their point of disembarkation together:

She let him take her hand when he came to sit down beside her, and smiled at him, only with rather a sad glance; she could say nothing to pain him till the moment of possible parting was nearer. And so they drank their cup of coffee together, and walked about the deck, and heard the captain's assurance that they should be in at Mudport by five o'clock, each with an inward burden; but in him it was an undefined fear, which he trusted to the coming hours to dissipate; in her it was a definite resolve on which she was trying silently to tighten her hold. . . . But a suppressed resolve will betray itself in the eyes, and Stephen became more and more uneasy as the day advanced, under the sense that Maggie had entirely lost her passiveness. . . . [E]ach time he looked at her, he gathered a stronger dread of the new, quiet sadness with which she met his eyes. And they were more and more silent.[11]

NINE

Eye Love You

Eye Contact in Relationships and Intimacy

*Lovers grow angry, are reconciled, entreat, thank,
make assignations, and in fine say everything,
with their eyes. . . .*

—MONTAIGNE[1]

The glance of love holds a mystery that poets throughout
the ages have tried to capture. Of course, no experience in
the world has spawned more love-struck, unsuccessful attempts
at poetic simile—"Your eyes are like a . . ." But a few master
poets have come closer than the rest of us in grasping the essential experience of gazing into a beloved's eye.

Wordsworth:

> *. . . those eyes,*
> *soft and capricious as a cloudless sky*

Whose azure depth their color emulates,
must needs be conversant with upward looks,
prayer's voiceless service.

Shakespeare, in *Romeo and Juliet:*

Her eye discourses; I will answer it.
I am too bold, 'tis not to me she speaks:
Two of the fairest stars in all the heaven,
Having some business, do entreat her eyes
To twinkle in their spheres till they return.
What if her eyes were there, they in her head?
The brightness of her cheek would shame those stars,
As daylight doth a lamp; her eyes in heaven
Would through the airy region stream so bright
That birds would sing and think it were not night.[2]

Some poets are so humbled by the ineffability of the eyes
of love that they choose to write about this ineffability and in-
comparability itself. Shakespeare, in Sonnet XVII:

If I could write the beauty of your eyes
And in fresh numbers number all your graces,
The age to come would say "This poet lies:
Such heavenly touches ne'er touch'd earthly faces."[3]

And this from Edmund Spenser:

Long-while I sought to what I might compare
Those powerful eyes, which lighten my dark sprite,
Yet find I nought on earth to which I dare
Resemble th'image of their goodly light.
Not to the sun: for they do shine by night;

Nor to the moon: for they are changed never;
Nor to the stars: for they have purer sight;
Nor to the fire: for they consume not ever;
Nor to the lightening: for they still persever;
Nor to the diamond: for they are more tender;
Nor unto crystal: for nought may them sever;
Nor unto glass: such baseness mought offend her;
Then to the Maker self they likest be,
Whose light doth lighten all that here we see.[4]

Just as the eyes propel us into mad embrace at the outset of love, so too—unfortunately—can that eye ardor fade after a couple has been together for a while, settling as it often can into complacency and listlessness.

Earlier chapters focused on the sizzling eye contact that can occur at the outset of a new romantic connection. In fact, most of my work with eye contact, through my Eye Gazing Parties, has focused on this side of eye contact.

In this chapter, however, I would like to talk about how loved ones can *rekindle* that eye flame that has kindled the imagination of poets for centuries.

I spoke on this topic with Gay and Kathyln Hendricks (www.hendricks.com), a couple well-known for teaching other couples intimacy skills through their workshops and books, including *Conscious Loving: The Journey to Co-Commitment.*

ELLSBERG: How can a couple bring intimacy in their communication and eye contact, if they've lost it, or perhaps never had it to begin with?

GAY HENDRICKS: Probably five thousand times in my career, I've been counseling a couple, and the woman will start talking—"I'm really concerned about our relationship and I want to make some changes . . ."—and as soon as she starts, the man's eyes are looking at the ceiling, looking at the floor, looking at his hands. Anywhere but her eyes.

Once things are underway, and there's some trust established in the session, I'll say, "Pause for a minute, Linda. Jim, I notice when she's talking, you don't look at her, or make eye contact—you're looking away." This is probably not politically correct to say, but I'd say that ninety-nine times out of a hundred, men don't look at women while women are talking. It's a very rare man that will actually appear to be interested in what she's saying. The rest of the time, they're doing a range of things, like thinking about something of theirs, or thinking judgmentally about what the other person is saying, or figuring out their rebuttal, or maybe just waiting until the other person stops talking.

We teach a course on listening, and one man in this course told me, "You know, I've realized that all my life, I've never listened. I've just been waiting until their mouths stop moving so I can talk."

When Katie and I were on the TV talk-show circuit, a talk-show host came up to me after the segment and said, "Can I ask you a question?"

"Sure," I said.

"Well, uh, I noticed when your wife is talking, you seemed to be paying attention to her. We have couples on here talking about relationships, and I've never seen anyone do that before. How do you do that?"

"Well, this is going to be a tough one," I said, "because I'm *actually interested* in what she says" [laughing].

ELLSBERG: Why do couples lose this eye intimacy?

GAY HENDRICKS: In the first year or so of life, you've really got two big psychological tasks. You've got to be open to nurturing and receiving. That's the first six months of life. And then in the second half of that year you're beginning to explore.

You're beginning to move away from that nurturing source. It's all about learning to let go into full intimacy, and also learning how to explore and let your exploration be OK.

This extends throughout our life. There are two pulsations: getting close to people, and getting separate and developing your own autonomy. It's a process of getting closer to and further away, closer to and further away. Ultimately, when you're able to do both—to be intimate, and yet fully yourself—that's as good as it gets.

Now, if that dance isn't going well, for one reason or another, the eyes become a way of managing that problem. A large part of whether you want to be close or separate is expressed and reflected through your eye contact.

KATHLYN HENDRICKS: Yes, we've noticed that in relationships, that's really all that's going on. People are either getting close, or getting separate. People have this illusion that it's a very harmonious dance—when I want to get close, you want to get close; when I want to get separate, you want to get separate. And it's never that way. I want to be close, but you've got something else you want to do—that's more often how it is.

This dance is reflected in the eyes—when someone is here physically, but you can tell in their eyes they are somewhere else emotionally or spiritually. All of that subtlety reads out in the eyes.

ELLSBERG: Do you ever incorporate practices or teachings specifically around helping couples with eye contact or eye gazing in your teachings?

KATHLYN HENDRICKS: Lots. We start out our couples course by having the couples be in eye contact, and then having them notice what is happening with their eye contact. Particularly as we ask them to let go of seeing their partner as an *improvement project* [laughing]. If I'm looking at you, I might be appreciating you, but what's most common is that I'm looking

at you thinking, "OK, if I could just fix the hair, and that shirt
. . . " [laughing] It's like, "Once I get you, I've got some plans
for *you*." We think a marriage license is a license to improve
each other!

So, we suggest various changes in attitude, and also changes
in breathing and movement, and see how that changes the eye
contact. The basic shift is from control to appreciation and
presence. Appreciating really brings presence, because so many
of us, for years and years and years, have had *being looked at* be
a source of criticism or judgment. In my family, if I were invisible, that was really good. But if I was noticed, I knew that
something was going to follow. "Are you going to wear that!?"
or "Stand up straight!"

Dismantling those filters is a lot of what goes on in creating a healthy flow of attention through the eyes. Eye contact is
one of the most precious ways we can give attention to another
person. It's such a great source of nourishment. Our work is to
help our clients and students let go of all the things they have
in the way of that, which keep them from getting and giving
nourishment just through their attention.

Presence is a major nutrient that people need lifelong. If
you think of babies, we just gaze at babies and look at them,
and we don't need to do anything; we just exchange gazes.
Then there's a certain point where people shift into "Now it's
time to *do*. We've got to get organized and do things in the
world." And they start organizing personas or roles so they can
get things done. But the quality of their presence suffers. Your
essence, who you really are, is so available just from gazing,
giving and receiving attention.

GAY HENDRICKS: From the perspective of a therapist,
people have "seeing filters" that cause them to see reality in a
certain way. For example, one common "seeing filter" is, as
Katie mentioned, "seeing to fix"—I'm looking at you as an

improvement project. Another common filter is "seeing to defend"—they see you and everything else in their life as a threat that they have to protect themselves from, often belligerently.

From the other direction, we also have things we're trying to ensure *others* don't see in *us*—what is it that I don't want you to see in me? If the eyes are indeed the windows to the soul, then how am I using my eyes to make sure you're not seeing a particular thing in me?

ELLSBERG: How do you teach your students to become more comfortable with this openness, vulnerability, and attention through the eyes?

KATHLYN HENDRICKS: To help people fully give attention without losing themselves, we teach our advanced students what's called the "loop of awareness." It's very simple but profound. The practice is to stay in eye contact, but be aware of your own body sensations. Then, while you're still in eye contact, put your attention on your partner. And then bring your attention back to yourself, and then back to your partner. It's a circle of awareness, and it allows people to have so much more freedom in their eye contact.

A lot of people really lose themselves in their eye contact. It's one of the big problems in a relationship: that one person just disappears into the other. Or they're afraid of disappearing into the other, so they never really let go. This helps them let go.

———————

In my own relationship experience, I have found that eye contact and intimacy are involved in a dance of co-causality. That is, more intimacy leads to more eye contact, and more eye contact leads to more intimacy, back and forth in this loop that the Hendrickses describe. Sadly, the reverse can be true as well for many couples: less eye contact leads to less intimacy, and less intimacy leads to less eye contact, down the negative spiral toward almost total isolation and alienation in the relationship.

If you're in a relationship now, whether you feel it's going wonderfully or needs a lot of work, intentional eye contact practices can be a powerful way to create a positive loop of ever-increasing intimacy and closeness.

Here is one practice I have found to be incredibly powerful:

For one month, both commit to starting each day (or each time you see each other, if you live separately), with two minutes of eye gazing.

We all live such hectic lives that it's obviously not always easy to do this. But when Jena and I have consistently carved out time for this first thing in the morning, the results have been dramatic. The rest of the day often flows smoothly with just a little reminder each morning, on an intensely direct, visceral level, of what's important in life: closeness, love, togetherness.

I can think of no better way to start the day then offering and receiving loving presence through our gaze.

Jena is an avid bicycle commuter in Manhattan. Each morning and evening, she careens between seemingly suicidal taxi drivers, randomly opening car doors, and multi-ton speeding trucks to get to and from her work. I sometimes feel, in relation to this pursuit, as my mother must have felt when I used to construct very large skateboard ramps in our driveway and fly off them at full speed.

I have been unable to dampen Jena's enthusiasm for her mode of commuting—she says it's one of her favorite parts of the day—though I have at least persuaded her to wear a helmet. Still, I am haunted by visions of the many ways it seems Jena's commute could all go wrong, with one speeding car. Along with these mental worst-case scenarios comes an awareness of the utter devastation I would feel if any of them turned into reality.

If she is nearby when one of these fear-visions haunts me, all of a sudden I see her with new eyes. If I have taken her for granted in any way during that day, even for a minute, I now send a massive "Thank you!" to the universe. For this moment, she is here in front of me, living, breathing, smiling. I walk over and give her a hug and kiss her on the forehead.

These mental excursions into the possibility of loss end up reminding me of the vastness of all we take for granted every day. For a few minutes, I appreciate the world anew, with the freshness and wonder of a baby's eyes. Zen Buddhists call it *beginner's mind*: experience of the openness of the world without preconceptions, without the filters and blinders —the "seeing filters," as Gay Hendricks calls them—that blunt our sensitivity to the mystery of the world around us and mire us in habituated, bored, dull perceptions of the world.

A man named Mike May was vaulted into seeing ordinary and quotidian experience with these beginner's eyes, baby's eyes, lover's eyes, in relation to a personal loss so massive few of us could even imagine it.

May enjoyed normal vision until the age of three, at which point he went completely blind due to a freak chemical accident. He went on to live a life more varied, successful, and interesting than most of us ever do, sighted or blind. In college, he worked for two years as a risk analyst for the CIA, the agency's first blind employee. An avid skier, he went on to set a world record in blind downhill skiing (which he still holds) and to win gold medals at the World Winter Games in Switzerland. He later founded a successful technology company to help the blind through GPS systems.

In 1999, a miraculous opportunity presented itself. Through a random encounter with an optometrist, May learned of an experimental new treatment involving stem-cell transplant surgery, which could potentially restore his sight after forty-three years of blindness. Only fifteen or twenty surgeons knew how to do the procedure. There was only a fifty-fifty chance it would work, and it involved taking strong medication afterwards with severe side effects, including a significant risk of cancer.

May was a happy man, in a wonderful marriage, with two children he loved, fulfilling work, and worldwide renown for his work with the blind. Should he take the risk of turning all of this into a misery of medical side effects, perhaps even dying of cancer, for a fifty-fifty chance of being able to lay eyes upon his wife and kids?

May opted to receive the treatment. It was successful.

The following is a description of an experience May had during his first year of vision after the surgery. It appears in a beautiful biography of May, *Crashing Through: The Extraordinary True Story of the Man Who Dared to See*, by Robert Kurson:

> [O]n a flight from Washington, DC, to Denver, May struck up a conversation with a young blonde woman seated next to him. Eventually, he told her about his surgery. She asked if he could see the color of her eyes. He replied that he could only do so from up close. She leaned forward and put her forehead just an inch from his. Her eyelashes fluttered up and down so close he believed he could feel their breeze. May had never before looked so closely into a stranger's eyes. He was overwhelmed with emotion and could not speak, not even to tell her that her eyes were a singular blue. He could only sit there and keep looking.
>
> Late that evening, he remained shaken from his encounter with the woman. Before he turned off the light next to his hotel bed, he opened his computer and typed, "This was a very intimate experience for me and I can't fathom how sighted

people go around seeing each other's eyes without being flustered too. I can understand a bit better now why so much is made of expressions in the eyes as it is talked about and written about passionately and poetically. I will certainly remember Ms. DC to Denver for introducing me to yet one more mystery of the sighted world."[5]

If your eyes for your loved one have become weary, if passion has faded into the mundane, would it be possible to remind yourself that there was a time when all the birds in all the trees seemed to sing just to you, simply because this one person returned your love? To remember that there was a time when only days or even hours away from this person seemed unbearable?

What if you were to imagine that you were unwillingly separated from this person for decades, as May was separated from his sight, and you have just been reunited through years of longing? If that were to happen, would you still look upon this person with eyes of banality?

When you were in your initial bloom of love—gaga-eyed with a childlike sense of wonder—the mere sight of your beloved could potentially open you to the infinite. Would it be possible, even for a moment, to gaze upon your loved one again with those fresh, wondering eyes—eyes awash in the miracle of life and love?

TEN

Gazing at the Divine

The Spiritual Side of Eye Contact

If there's one proverb about the eyes that almost everyone knows, as we've seen in this book, it's "The eyes are the window to the soul." While up until now this book has mostly been about practical applications of eye contact for business, sales, dating, deepening relationships, and so forth, we can see by this simple saying that there is something deeper. The one piece of commonly disseminated folk wisdom about the eyes and eye contact doesn't talk about sales or flirting. It goes straight to the spiritual; it talks about our *souls*.

When a child is misbehaving, and you say "Look at me when I'm talking to you!" would you be satisfied if that child looked at your feet or your hands? Of course not. What you mean by "look at me" is "look into my eyes." We identify our eyes with our *selves*, our essence, our soul.

The spiritual side of eye contact was made most obvious to me when I came across a stunning little volume entitled *The Spiritual Practices of Rumi: Radical Techniques for Beholding the Divine*, by Will Johnson.[1] Anyone familiar with the life of

Rumi—by some reckonings now the most widely read poet in the West—will know that the most important event in his life was meeting Shams-i-Tabriz, a wandering Sufi mystic.

Shams was a spiritual gadfly, who—like the cynic philosopher Diogenes over fifteen hundred years earlier—apparently encouraged people to give up their ego attachments by *insulting* their egos, either directly or with impolite, antisocial behavior. As would be expected, he was not well loved, and he frequently moved elsewhere when a given populace rejected him.

At the same time, Rumi was a preacher of Sufism in his community of Konya (in modern-day Turkey) and a teacher in a beloved madrassa (religious school) founded by his father. Rumi was, at this stage in his life, not unlike some small-city preachers one might meet today: well loved and respected among a local community, but hardly destined for immortality.

Then, in 1244, the most important event happened in Rumi's life: he met Shams. Whereas others dismissed Shams as a near lunatic, an instantaneous electrical spark occurred between the two spiritual seekers. Soon after, they holed themselves up in a small prayer cell and spent ninety days there together.

Rumi was a transformed man when he emerged from that cell. Whereas before he had *taught* mysticism, now he seemed to *embody* it, to radiate it from his pores. He seemed much less interested in the pieties and formalities of his professorship and preaching, and much more interested in direct experience of ecstatic union with the divine.

It was also during this time that Rumi began writing his poetry—much of it suffused with his feelings of divine merging with and love for Shams—bequeathing to posterity a body of poetry Rumi called *The Works of Shams of Tabriz*, one of the great literary treasures of history.

Needless to say, not all of Rumi's devout students and colleagues were thrilled with this transformation from upright preacher and professor to unbridled mystic poet. Controversy swirled in the community about what exactly had transpired, and it continues among scholars to this day. What on earth were they doing in there? Were they meditating? Praying? Dancing? Drinking? Making love?

In *The Spiritual Practices of Rumi*, Will Johnson reviews and interprets the poetry and prose Rumi produced following the ninety-day period and makes a compelling case that what the two seekers were doing during most of that time was *gazing into each other's eyes, silently.*

"I believe—and the poetry bears witness to this belief—that they continued, behind the closed doors of their retreat room, to hold each other's gaze for long periods at a time, relaxing and surrendering into the practice, dissolving together into a shared awareness of the great ground of being."[2]

Johnson's argument for this view is more detailed than I can spell out here (and for anyone interested in the spiritual dimensions of eye contact, I couldn't recommend the volume more enthusiastically), but in many ways the main argument is presented in the actual lines of Rumi that Johnson selects and presents in his book:

> I said to him, "Your zeal is great,
> But your eyes look so small and slanted.
> If you know the secret, just come out with it
> and tell me!"
>
> "My eyes are not small," he replied,
> "But the road to the secret is indeed narrow.
> Just keep looking at my narcissus eyes,
> And try to find a road from them to that which
> you seek." [3]

Here's another example:

Both our sets of eyes became drunk,
Utterly intoxicated by the promise of Union.
O my God!
What is this union of eye to eye?![4]

Another volume of Rumi's poetry, *The Glance: Songs of Soul-Meeting*, collected and translated by Coleman Barks, explores similar themes. In Rumi's lines, we again see the ecstasy he experienced, allowing himself to dissolve in the gaze of his spiritual consort, Shams:

I see my beauty in you. I become
a mirror that cannot close its eyes

to your longing. My eyes wet with
yours in the early light. My mind

every moment giving birth, always
conceiving, always in the ninth

month, always the come-point. How
do I stand this? We become these

words we say, a wailing sound moving
out into the air. These thousands of

worlds that rise from nowhere, how
does your face contain them? I'm

a fly in your honey, then closer, a
moth caught in flame's allure, then

empty sky stretched out in homage.[5]

I interviewed the translator of these poems, Coleman Barks. Barks is widely considered the preeminent translator of Rumi into English. Huston Smith, scholar of comparative religion and author of the classic *The World's Religions*, said of him: "If Rumi is the most-read poet in America today, Coleman Barks is in good part responsible."

I pointed out that I was struck by the obvious erotic energy expressed in the gaze between Rumi and Shams, almost as if they were romantic lovers.

BARKS: We know very well that something sexual gets transmitted in the eyes. Every movie star knows that. But the transformation of that into something closer to a deep friendship occurred between Rumi and Shams. There's an alchemy that goes on.

It's all love poetry. That's all Rumi's poetry is. But it's trying to expand that into a new place—the synapse of lovers dissolves. He says, "If you see the beloved everywhere, then you, the lover, are the veil. But when living itself becomes the friend, lovers disappear."

I got a call from Hallmark, and they wanted to put Rumi's poems on their cards. I said, "But this is the love that obliterates the lovers." She was quiet for a while. Then she said, "Is there a holiday for that?" [laughing]. I guess that would be every day. This is not Valentine's, the kind of love we're talking about.

I don't think you can call it erotic. Maybe you can't even call it love. Maybe we need a new word for it. In Persian, there are about ten or twenty words for all the different kinds of love. But we don't have that many.

What Rumi and Shams experienced is definitely beyond romance. And I think it's beyond gender. It's beyond age, and it's maybe beyond touch. It's a meeting in the heart or the soul. Whatever those things mean—his love poetry is an exploration of that region.

It's what William James calls the "oceanic feeling," when the dewdrop melts into the ocean, and you feel a great interconnectedness, like you are part of the ocean, and the ocean swims inside of you, and you're moving in it, and you're connecting with everything in it that way. And that's the feeling of ecstasy, and also the feeling of longing, because even though you are still in it, you still long for it. . . . Any questions? [laughing]

I also talked about the spiritual side of eye gazing with Will Johnson (www.embodiment.net), author of the book I mentioned above, *The Spiritual Practices of Rumi*. This book originally clued me in to the deeper spiritual dimensions of eye contact.

ELLSBERG: What is it specifically about eye contact that is so powerful for creating these deep states of spiritual awareness and connection?

JOHNSON: My honest answer is that I have no idea, other than to know that it *does* have that powerful effect on us. The connection is palpable—it's like two wires touching, with sparks, and then you get electricity. You both feel it. Of course, we're talking about times when people come together who are really drawn to each other—that's the deepest.

Anybody can do this with anybody, and you're going to have different experiences. And you will start to dissolve into each other to some degree. But when there is a special interest, or intrigue, or attraction, that's when it can go the deepest.

When eyes connect with each other, some kind of link is established. And what that link apparently does is allow the limited, isolated, separate sense of self to start melting. And we just fall into "being with" our partner—this great place that Rumi calls "the consciousness of union." Different traditions talk about this. Buddhists talk about "nondual" states of awareness, and the Sufis talk about *fana*, or annihilation of consciousness of the self. This is what we experience in the deepest reaches of gazing.

ELLSBERG: What is the relationship between this deep gazing where you completely dissolve into an ecstatic state and lose awareness of the limited ego, on the one hand, and your everyday experiences with eye contact on the other hand, say talking with someone at a cocktail party? Do you see any connection between those two experiences at all?

JOHNSON: Yes and no. The nature of gazing practice is about dissolving into the highest states. It's not going to happen quickly. Yes, the connection is always there in any form of eye contact: it's amazing in the moment, it's amazing in the next moment, and every moment it deepens.

But if you try the practice for hours, day after day, you get to a place where there's a beautiful opening and a dissolving, and you think you can't go any further; you are in complete union with your partner. And the next morning, you wake up and try it again, and you go deeper.

———

Annie Lalla, my friend whom we met in Chapter 3, described a similar experience to me:

LALLA: There's a point where you're having eye contact— if you know someone well or really trust them—and you relinquish your sense of otherness with that person. So it's not like "You're looking into my eyes," or "I'm looking into yours." There is just eye contact happening.

And this only happens with prolonged eye contact—I'll actually see myself diving into the other person, and if my imagination is particularly animated, I'll be able to climb in and look out at the world through their eyes. That allows the boundary between us to really soften, and there's this space where I don't know who's who. There's just the gaze. I am the gaze, they are the gaze. You have to feel really safe to do that.

———

Of course, both Lalla and Johnson emphasized that this soul-melting typically happens only with someone you already know and trust.

JOHNSON: Deep melting into each other is one extreme. But here we are living in a world where people don't even look at each other—where it's actually taboo to look at each other. So if you're standing at a checkout counter, and you just open with a simple gaze and a relaxed presence—that may be the other person's initial opening. You have actually taken a risk to "draw first" and be vulnerable with that person. It could be the only vulnerability he or she has seen all day, in an otherwise very impersonal environment. Because when it comes to gazing, we're always waiting for the other person to "draw first" and give us permission.

So, this is taboo in our culture, and yet we're all yearning for it. You see the yearning in little babies in strollers in the supermarkets who catch your eye, and they just can't take their eyes off yours. You see it with lovers. You see it with parents and their kids. It's utterly natural. We're all seeking this communal experience of union. And it's available to us.

Having said that, you have to recognize that you have to be very sensitive around these issues. When two people make eye contact, you both open only as far as the person who is able to open the least is able to go. So it isn't necessarily this huge dissolve with everyone. And quite frankly, it isn't appropriate, say, for the checkout girl at the supermarket to stand there and dissolve her consciousness into a bliss state. I'm not going to go into a board meeting in an ecstatic state and expect results!

ELLSBERG: How do you guide people into becoming comfortable with gazing?

JOHNSON: I'll tell them just to start looking at the other person. Let your eyes look at the eyes of the other person, and see what happens. Now often what happens is that people get giggly. Or they get kind of nervous. Because what you feel is so different than what we're used to in our day-to-day lives. Some people will giggle nervously, or just think, "Whoooa, what is going on?"

Generally, what I tell people is, stay with that feeling, and keep on surrendering to it. Just relax. Relax and accept it. Know that whatever you're experiencing is OK, whatever you're feeling is OK. In fact, it's the perfect thing for you to be feeling. Just keep accepting what comes up, and continue to do the practice.

That's the front-door approach, and that's very confrontational for some people, because you're asking them to do something that is essentially taboo in our culture. The back-door approach is that I'll often sit with someone and say, "OK, let's just start off by letting ourselves hear the sounds around us." After a moment, I say "Now let yourself just take a look at the whole of your visual field." After they have accustomed to that, I say, "Now let yourself just start feeling sensations in your body."

Nine times out of ten, if I talk with someone like that, at the end of those three awarenesses—audio field, visual field, and tactile field—they're looking right at me.

Ultimately, what you have to tell people is this: "Relax and trust. Relax and trust your experience." We're so conditioned not to trust our experience. This is all about direct experience. Direct experience of something that is very beautiful and extraordinary—if we can give ourselves permission to open it. I'm very clear that Rumi is just wanting to give us back our birthright.

Michael Murphy: Eye Gazing as Mystical Union

To understand the role of eye contact, and in particular the practice of deep eye gazing in spiritual practice, I decided to ask many different spiritual seekers and teachers for their thoughts.

I talked with Michael Murphy, founder of the famous Esalen Institute in Big Sur, California (www.esalen.org), which was an epicenter for the development of transpersonal and humanistic psychology, and the human potential movement in general, in the sixties and seventies. Murphy is known as a father of these fields (or now, grandfather, as he is a vibrant seventy-eight).

Over lunch at a restaurant overlooking the San Francisco Bay in Sausalito, Murphy shared with me an extremely erudite explication of eye contact and eye gazing.

MURPHY: In my book *The Future of the Body,* I talk about different recurring practices that either are deliberately cultivated or arise spontaneously in various spiritual traditions. These are modalities that facilitate liberating insights and promote personal growth. Eye gazing is one of these.

And as you might expect with practices that recur in different formats, they have a history, for example in Tibetan tantric practice. Tantra is a meta-theory that spread across Asia, from India to Tibet, China, and Japan, and is far broader than the sublimated sexual act. Tantra is that vision of existence that says that the divine is immanent [in the here and now] as well as transcendent. As soon as you make that move in a contemplative tradition, you then engage all our parts: body, mind, and soul. And within Tantra, eye gazing sometimes appears as a practice.

The more incarnational a practice is—taking into account the body as well as the soul and mind—the more something like eye gazing comes up. And why? There are probably many reasons, among them one that the great psychologist Erik Erikson helps us understand. He maintained that basic eye contact with the mother is important for a child's healthy development. That is the case, he believed, because to be seen is to be known. To be seen, and to see, is primal—particularly when you're a child.

What Erikson said, and others have pointed out, is that a child knows right away if he or she is loved and seen. We seem to be genetically predisposed to know this. To be seen is to be loved—because if someone refuses to look at you, this is a kind of ostracism, a banishment from love and acceptance, a signal of hostility or disgust. Some people have mothers and fathers who barely look at them.

People come to Esalen and suddenly, while eye gazing, they're seen and accepted for who they are. And they realize, "I really am all right." It's so poignant. Sometimes they break down, and you want to cry just watching them. If they've never been loved as infants, they're carrying that weight all their life, and in a practice like eye gazing they can let it go.

It's a hell of a process, like reading a great and wonderful book. To read the book of another person's soul. It's fascinating. Sheer discovery. Why go to Paris? Why Florence? Or India? Why do some people skydive, or climb mountains? This is to expand their horizon. Through eye gazing this happens just sitting still, seeing the depths of another person. A new world appears, with vistas you hadn't imagined. And healing. And liberation. What an extraordinary, unexpected experience!

If we want to take this even further, into the realm of metaphysics and mysticism, you can speculate that through eye gazing you reenact the secret of all secrets. You're in Rumi country. One of his poems says, "For a thousand years, I knocked at the Beloved's door, and when it opened at long last, I saw I was knocking from the inside." It's an inversion: you become one with the beloved, and that is who you were from the start.

This is also the ultimate idea in the Indian Vedanta, where Atman, our deepest subjectivity, our truest self, is Brahman, the omnipresent reality. So Brahman-Atman means that our deepest subjectivity is one with everything. I have heard people say, "Eye gazing has permanently changed my life. I know who I am, now that I know who you are, and that you and I are one." To me, that sounds like the ancient mystical, metaphysical insight, the deepest reason to engage in spiritual practice.

———————

At this point, my mother, Patricia, who was also at the meal with Murphy, broke in.

PATRICIA ELLSBERG: In eye gazing, you fall in love, but it's not necessarily with the other's personality. It's with something much more profound. It's almost beyond the person.

I've done this practice in workshops, and I fall in love with everybody! Even if I don't particularly *like* everybody! [laughing]. I mean, I may not even want to go to lunch with that person—but I see his or her deepest beauty, and I can feel my own beauty through that. It's so powerful, and it's absolutely ecstatic.

MURPHY: You ought to quote her on this! [laughing]. These are good quotes! Beautiful. That's a much simpler way of saying what I was trying to say. You reestablish your connection with the ultimate, the beloved. Or Atman–Brahman, to use impersonal language. And that impersonal aspect gives it breadth and power and stability, so that you can handle more of the personal.

———————

Our wide-ranging discussion soon moved to a different topic: the darker or more dangerous side of eye gazing.

MURPHY: You don't want to be too soft or Pollyannaish in your writing about this. You should write about the shadows, too. There is a dark side. When you do these things superficially, a lot of people have "looser hinges" than others. Some people become disoriented in this practice. Their doors of perception swing open wildly. I would say what you've got going here—this eye gazing thing—you're playing with dynamite.

You can see some very creepy things. Truly deeply creepy,

and it becomes disturbing. This person across from you can scare you, and with good reason.

————

Later in my research for this book, I came across a haunting rendition from Ralph Waldo Emerson's *The Conduct of Life*, reprinted in the Appendix, which suggests that Emerson had seen similar dark potential in the meeting of the eyes of strangers:

> *We look into the eyes to know if this other form is another self, and the eyes will not lie, but make a faithful confession what inhabitant is there. The revelations are sometimes terrific. The confession of a low, usurping devil is there made, and the observer shall seem to feel the stirring of owls, and bats, and horned hoofs, where he looked for innocence and simplicity.*[6]

Murphy continued on this theme.

MURPHY: Let's say you eye gaze with someone without having a long history with them. And suddenly you realize this person is just trouble—real trouble—but sexy. God knows what got connected at your Eye Gazing Parties! [laughing] I could tell you many stories on this. You know the old expression? "If you're going to dance with a bear, get ready to dance all night."

Eye to Eye with the Divine: *Darsan* and *Shaktipat*

In Calcutta, a young western spiritual seeker named Sera Beak wakes up at 3:30 a.m. and takes a taxi to the far outskirts of the sprawling city to see a temple called Dakineshwar, one of the main temples honoring the goddess Kali.

She expects to find a serene scene at such an early hour, but when she finally arrives after a long taxi ride, she instead finds a large crowd gathered. It appears that a fight is breaking out in the center of the crowd.

"I see a pushing match, almost a fight, erupting among the center of the crowd," Beak told me. "I had no idea what these people were pushing and shoving about."

It turns out they were hoping to receive *darsan* from the statue of Kali at the temple.

Beak, a Harvard-trained student of mysticism and comparative religion, author of *The Red Book: A Deliciously Unorthodox Approach to Igniting Your Divine Spark*, and one of the most intrepid spiritual seekers and wanderers I've met (www.serabeak.com), explained this concept to me.

BEAK: *Darsan,* in Hindu tradition, is the idea that an icon, a statue, a photograph, or even a living person embodies elements of the sacred, so when you are looking at these, it is not only important to see them and hold them in your vision, but it's even more important that they see you—it's the divine seeing you through their eyes.

That morning in Calcutta, when I finally got in close enough to the statue of Kali and saw what all the pushing and shoving was about, I realized that they weren't just wanting to see the statue. They were trying to position themselves directly in front of this icon so Kali could see them. Once they got her *darsan,* then they were good and they could go. It was a very different experience than being in America, where you might crowd around some famous person just to catch a glimpse. These people actually wanted Kali to see *them.*

When I was studying among Tibetan Buddhists in India, I spent time with people creating statues of the different Buddhas and deities, and *thangkas,* paintings depicting mythological scenes, to be hung in monasteries. And what I found was that they would wait to draw or sculpt the eyes until the very end—because when they draw the eyes, that is when the painting or statue comes alive and becomes imbued with the divine and the spiritual.

A lot of times what they'll do is create a whole ceremony. It might have taken them a year to create this statue or painting, and people will come and they'll have chants rituals and incense, and then the artist draws on the eyes. A lot of times they'll hold a mirror so that the eyes will look back at the crowd—and it's considered that the divine is looking at you.

———————

Beak reminded me of a similar, related concept in the Hindu tradition, *shaktipat*, the direct, face-to-face transmission of divine energy from spiritual teacher to student. While *shaktipat* can occur simply in the presence of the teacher, the most powerful *shaktipat*—not surprisingly—comes during direct eye contact with the teacher.

Beak tells me of an experience she had while waiting to receive her *shaktipat* from Amma, the famous "hugging saint" of India. So strong is Amma's spiritual energy that people travel all over the world, and wait in line ten or fifteen hours, to have the opportunity to hug her for a few moments. She often hugs up to 50,000 people a day, in stretches of up to twenty hours. Beak was one of these people.

BEAK: I remember standing in line to receive her hug, and the people in front of me have to be kneeling down because they're so close. And she looked at me as she was hugging someone and talking in their ear. I started sweating, I started crying—before I even went into her arms. She felt like an embodiment of the divine feminine, in the flesh, looking out at me with those eyes.

Eye Gazing as a Spiritual Practice

By now, I hope you have tried gazing into a friend or loved one's eyes in one of the exercises in this book. If you have, you probably noticed something very quickly: the mind wanders.

What does she think of me? What does that look mean? Does she like me? What does he see in my eyes? Does he think I'm fat?
     Or, if your mind doesn't wander in the direction of wondering about your eye gazing partner and the meaning of your shared gaze, it might instead wander in the direction of daily obligations and tasks:

Darn, I forgot the milk! What time do I have to get up tomorrow? Oh no, there was that unpaid phone bill sitting on the kitchen table!
     And on, and on. Sometimes it can feel as though our minds are conspiring to get us to focus on anything *but* the experience we are having in the present moment: gazing into another's eyes.
     This is where we begin to see the *meditative* quality of eye gazing. There are probably as many definitions of meditation as there are practitioners. I do not consider myself a master meditator. But I have been meditating fairly consistently since I was fifteen, when I first took a course in (where else?) Berkeley, California. My first course was on Transcendental Meditation, the style created by Maharishi Mahesh Yogi and popularized in the sixties by his most famous disciples, the Beatles. I later switched to a form of Buddhist meditation known as vipassana, as taught by Western Buddhist teacher Jack Kornfield. Over the years, I developed my own style of meditation just for me, fusing various aspects of what I had learned over the years.
     The understanding that I came to as a result of my admittedly

limited experience is that meditation is, above all, a form of mental training. Just as we can train the body to act in a coordinated, disciplined, elegant way during some physical activity such as dancing, swimming, or playing soccer, rather than flopping about chaotically and clumsily, we can also train the mind to respond in a coordinated, disciplined, and elegant way to life experience itself.

When left to its own devices, without training, the mind tends toward chaos—the barrage of anxious thinking described above. Mihaly Csikszentmihalyi, the former head of the psychology department at the University of Chicago, captures this dynamic beautifully in his celebrated book *Flow: The Psychology of Optimal Experience*:

> [W]hen we are left alone, with no demands on attention, the basic disorder of the mind reveals itself. With nothing to do, it begins to follow random patterns, usually stopping to consider something painful or disturbing. Unless a person knows how to give order to his or her thoughts, attention will be attracted to whatever is most problematic in the moment: it will focus on some real or imagined pain, on recent grudges, or long-term frustrations. Entropy is the normal state of consciousness—a condition that is neither useful nor enjoyable."[7]

Meditation, in my view, is the "giving order to thoughts" that Csikszentmihalyi mentions. Of course, he lists many other ways to do this in his book, including sports training, dancing, sex, yoga, work, martial arts, appreciation of music, art, and food, reading, conversation, poetry, and science and other mental disciplines. For me, though, meditation is the most direct way to mental focus, because it is the one activity for which mental discipline is the object of the activity itself, not just a pleasurable byproduct.

So what is meditation? It is the simple act of consciously *bringing your awareness back*. When your mind wanders into chaos—as it invariably will, along the lines that Csikszentmihalyi describes—you bring your awareness (or attention, or focus) *back*. What you bring your awareness back *to* is what distinguishes various forms of meditation. In some forms, such as Transcendental Meditation, you bring it back to a specific word, called a "mantra." In other forms, such as various branches of Zen, you bring it back to the breath, or to a series of counting. In vipassana, you bring it back to the sensations in your body. In other forms, you bring it back to a chant or to an image.

To this list of meditation forms, I would like to add eye gazing, which Rumi and Shams developed into a high spiritual art more than eight hundred years ago. Eye gazing as a meditation is not a lot different from the prolonged eye gazing exercise I recommended at the beginning of Chapter 2. However, there are some additional considerations I recommend to anyone seeking to expand spiritual awareness through gazing.

How to Experience Eye Gazing as a Spiritual Practice

1. Choose a partner you are very close to: for example, your spouse or significant other, or a close friend or family member. It should be someone you are very comfortable with. You do *not* want to be worrying if this person is judging you during the meditation. Ideally, it is someone with whom you share a great deal of fondness, affection, or love.
2. Pay attention to your environment. In the other eye gazing experiences you may have tried throughout the book, your surroundings have not been that

important. But for eye gazing as meditation, you should select a quiet place where you will not be disturbed. Turn off cell phones, silence ringers, make sure no one is going to barge in.

3. You may like to eye gaze in silence, or you may find that music enhances it. Try it both ways and see which way you like best. When you do use music, make sure it is not too loud, as that can distract from the experience.

4. Lighting should be atmospheric, but definitely not too low. In other words, no fluorescent lights, but not just a few candles, either. Warm light accented by a few candles is perfect. Many people who try gazing for the first time err on the side of too little light, in an attempt to be romantic. The trouble is that you are actually looking at something—namely, your partner's eyes—so without enough light your eyes will begin to feel the strain. And you won't catch all the subtleties in your partner's eyes, either.

5. Since this is someone you are already close and familiar with, I recommend sitting as close together as possible—it enhances the experience immeasurably. Try sitting cross-legged in front of each other, with knees touching. Or sit next to each other on a couch and face each other. For this experience I recommend against sitting at a table, as the whole point is union and togetherness, and the table can feel like a wall between you.

Once you have these elements in place, gaze in just the same way we've already learned, with both of your eyes looking into one of your partner's eyes. (You can switch which of your partner's eyes you look at.)

As I noted earlier in this chapter, you will most likely begin to notice your mind wandering very quickly—to the laundry, the bills, your co-worker's snide comment today, and so on.

This is where your chance to practice meditation comes in. Simply notice these thoughts, and let them pass, without getting caught up in them or even judging yourself for having them. ("I'm supposed to be *meditating*, not having all these thoughts!") Having thoughts, and letting them pass, *is* meditation.

Whenever you notice yourself having gone down a train of thought—which at the beginning will be quite frequently—simply bring your attention back to your partner's gaze.

Another thing to keep in mind while engaging in a prolonged practice of gazing is to not get overly caught up in your own interpretations of the other person's emotions or facial expressions. *What is the other person feeling? Thinking? Experiencing?* We can get tremendously mired in thinking about these questions, rather than just *feeling* the other person without necessarily putting words or concepts to his or her emotional state.

In relation to this point, I am reminded of the famous "Afghan Girl" photograph, which appeared on the cover of the June 1985 *National Geographic*. Sharbat Gula was approximately thirteen when she was photographed by Steve McCurry in a Pakistani refugee camp during the Soviet war in Afghanistan. Her piercing green eyes in the photograph are—after the eyes of the Mona Lisa—probably the most widely recognized eyes in a work of visual art.

One could spend hours trying to discern what is being expressed by those eyes, by what is going on in her emotions and mind as she is photographed. Fear? Anger? Reproach? Innocence? Lost innocence? All of these at once? This aspect of the photograph is often compared to the Mona Lisa. As in the painting, it's very difficult to characterize what the expression is. Yet, both works seem to communicate so much, without us being able to pin down exactly what.

I asked McCurry why this photograph in particular—as

compared to thousands of others we see each year—continues to haunt us long after the first time we see it. "That ambiguity, that mystery," he said. "We can think 'This is what it must mean, this is what's going on.' We can make up stories in our mind. But ultimately, we have no idea."

Instead of trying to pin down your gazing partner's expression and attach meaning and stories to it, see if you can simply experience the expression, let it impact you viscerally, affect your whole being, without interpreting or categorizing your partner's expression. That is when you start to see the subtlety and mystery of the gaze.

Incorporating the Breath

The link between breathing and spirituality is a well-known theme among those seriously devoted to a spiritual practice. Indeed, even the word "spirit" comes from the Latin *spiritus,* breathing. Every Eastern spiritual path that I'm aware of, including yoga, t'ai chi, chi gung, Buddhist meditation of every stripe, and tantra, places strong emphasis on breath as a path to tranquility and inner calm.

There may be many reasons why this connection between breath and spirituality exists, but most likely one of them is the direct, physiological effect that slow breathing has on counteracting the well-known "fight-or-flight" response to stress. The fight-or-flight response involves an activation of the sympathetic nervous system—including the release of adrenaline and the "stress hormone" cortisol—in response to a perceived danger or threat, or the need to adjust to change in the environment. Instantly, heart and respiratory rate increase, blood flow to the muscles increases, and a host of other reactions occurs throughout our physiology, getting us ready to, well, fight or flee.

In the late sixties and early seventies, Harvard cardiologist Herbert Benson hypothesized that the chronic activation of fight-or-flight in response to low-level yet ever-present stressors within the modern urban environment might be contributing to poor health outcomes such as high blood pressure and heart disease.

This was considered blasphemy at the time, as the view that mental, psychological, or emotional states might affect health was considered quackery by the medical establishment. But he pressed on, conducting studies of practitioners of Transcendental Meditation. He found incontrovertible evidence that meditation reversed the fight-or-flight response, leading to a decrease in sympathetic nervous activity, including lowered heart rate, respiratory rate, and blood lactate levels and an increase in the highly relaxing alpha brainwaves.

What's more, he showed that consistently counteracting the effects of the fight-or-flight response in our bodies leads to significant improvement in conditions including hypertension, heart disease, anxiety, depression, fatigue, insomnia, chronic pain, and many others. Benson dubbed this dynamic *The Relaxation Response* in his seminal 1975 book by that name. It is now common wisdom that relaxation and a decrease in stress lead to improved health outcomes across a wide range of conditions, and we largely have Benson to thank for that awareness.

There are many ways to evoke the Relaxation Response. In his book, Benson focuses on forms of meditation in which a word or mantra is repeated. (Interestingly, he also lists "a fixed gaze" as one of the ways to invoke the Relaxation Response.[8]

Yet virtually any form of meditation, spiritual practice, or any other activity in which concentration is focused—the "flow" state described by Csikszentmihalyi—is likely to have this effect. Deep, slow breathing counteracts the shallow, rapid breathing of the fight-or-flight response and is thus widely considered by experts in the field of mind-body medicine as one of the fastest ways to relax, de-stress, and counteract the fight-or-flight response. I know from my own experience that deep, slow breathing is the most direct way to short-circuit my mental chatter and evoke a state of mental calm and relaxation. The yogis who invented this technique millennia ago were definitely on to something.

If you want to incorporate this powerful tool of breath within eye gazing, here is how:

1. Practice extremely slow, deep breaths as you gaze with your partner. See if you can prolong the in-breath to last for a count of ten. Hold the breath for a few seconds. Then prolong the out-breath for a count of ten as well. You will be amazed at how quickly this extremely slow breathing can bring you into a state of meditative calm. Don't worry if you don't reach ten seconds on each inhale and exhale. Even a count of five for each will noticeably calm you down.

2. Once you are comfortable with these long, slow breaths, you can try something called the "three-part breath." (In yoga practice, this is called *dirga pranayama*.) The idea is simple. Inhale deeply, filling your belly. Once your belly is full, let your rib cage expand and fill with air. Once your rib cage is full with air, let your upper chest fill with air. Then, on the exhale, let the air out in reverse order. First let all of the air out of the upper chest, then the rib cage, then the belly.

3. With or without this three-part breath, try synchronizing your breaths. You can either discuss this beforehand, or—even more electric—let it arise

naturally. Breathing in synch, on both the inhale
and the exhale, adds another layer of connectedness
and union between you and your partner. It can
feel truly exalted, as if the boundaries between you
are dissolving and you are becoming one living,
breathing organism together—two lungs of the same
being.

Rumi and Shams apparently spent hours upon hours, even
days, simply gazing into each other's eyes. So you can push the
limits here a bit. Try ten minutes at first. If that goes well, in
the same session or on another occasion, push it up to fifteen
minutes, then twenty, then half an hour.

What you will notice in these prolonged gazing sessions,
as in all meditation, is that at some point your thoughts will
begin to subside to a certain degree. And what's left is just pure
awareness. You, your partner's eyes, your partner—joined together in a moment of pure beholding: no judgment, no evalu-
ation, no worries, just eyes and souls meeting.

Even one moment of this pure awareness, this dissolution of
the normal boundaries that separate us, can feel ecstatic. Five
seconds, ten seconds, thirty seconds of it could feel like one of
the most exalted experiences of your life.

Again, do not seek this state. Do not get angry if you don't
"achieve" it. Worrying about it makes all that much more elusive. States of meditative awareness arise on their own, eventually, if you do the practice. It all sounds very paradoxical, but
not worrying about the practice is, in some sense, the very essence of the practice itself.

As you continue this practice—probably not on your first
session, but perhaps your third or fourth—you may find that
your habitual and patterned thoughts have subsided to such a
degree that you can begin to introduce more positive thoughts

in their absence. When you have reached a relative state of calm in the meditation practice, experiment with adding positive thoughts about your partner.

You could, for example:

- Imagine that you are looking not at a set of eyes, or a human body, but a human *soul*, full of emotions, longing, desires, frustrations, and joys. These emotions are always present in your partner to some degree or another. See if you can pick up on all of them. See the essential *dignity* of your partner.

- Imagine your partner's heart full of love. Feel her desire to live a life full of love, both giving and receiving. In your heart, wish well for this person. Wish that she may experience the love all humans desire so strongly. Imagine her feeling that love already. This is a version of Buddhist meditation called *metta*, or "loving kindness" meditation.

- Imagine the space between you and your partner. Imagine yourselves dissolving into each other, the separation erasing, becoming one being, not two, unified by breath and gaze.

ELEVEN

Going Deeper

A Graduate Degree in Eye Contact

We've learned all kinds of techniques for improving your eye contact. All of them are valuable and will lead to noticeable differences in the quality of your eye contact and to impressive results in your relationships, from the professional to the personal, from the casual to the most intimate.

However, in all my experience and study of eye contact, I've come to believe that the way to truly excel in eye contact—at a level where people sometimes tell you that they feel they're melting into your eyes—has nothing to do with techniques. It has nothing to do with which eye you look into, for how long, and at what distance. It has everything to do with your relation to *yourself*.

What do I mean by this? Let's step back a minute. Most everyone feels some discomfort with eye contact at first, from mild to extreme. What is all this discomfort about, really? Why are we so nervous about meeting eyes with a stranger, or even a loved one?

The more I've thought about it, the more obvious to me the answer has become. It's because, as we've seen in this book, the eyes give others immediate access to our emotional states. If you are feeling sad, the other person will know. If you are feeling angry, the other person will know.

More importantly, if you are not feeling right with yourself—if there's some part of you that you're ashamed of, that you don't accept fully, that you're not comfortable with—the other person will know. They may not have a conscious feeling, "Oh, this person isn't comfortable with some aspect of himself." But their bodies will know. Their animal instinct will kick in.

When we meet eyes with another person, we are naked, emotionally speaking. All of you—the good, the bad, and the ugly—is out and about, available and accessible to the other person.

So, whatever part of ourselves that is not totally settled, whatever part of ourselves we're not right about—we are bound to feel exposed and shy about letting others see that in our gaze. *That's* where our hesitancy and fear about eye contact come from.

The way to deeper eye contact, and to improved relations with others in general, is to accept ourselves as whole human beings, to accept our successes and failures, our areas of brilliance and our deep shortcomings. Accept it all and love it all.

I'm not suggesting that you should never act to change or improve yourself. If you have a drinking problem, or you want to quit smoking or stop overspending, or your doctor tells you that you need to go easy on your junk-food habit *or else*, I'm not suggesting you simply resign yourself to these problems for the rest of your life. I'm simply suggesting that you recognize that these shortcomings are part of you as much as your areas of brilliance, just as a child struggling with emotional problems or difficult behavior is still a part of your family. Ideally, you will still love this child even as you help him or her grow up.

Likewise, I suggest that you love and accept all the parts of your inner emotional family even as you help some of them mature and cause you less trouble.

If you come to a place of self-acceptance, cleansing yourself of shame, you'll have no problem looking someone right in the eyes with the deepest tenderness and vulnerability. If you're feeling sad, or disappointed, or frustrated, you'll still feel comfortable showing others that emotion, letting them into your world, because you're right with those emotions in yourself.

Of course, the benefits of self-acceptance go way beyond eye contact. Better eye contact is more like a surprise, a nice side effect of self-acceptance. The main benefit is that you'll feel better and be able to love deeper. But this book is about eye contact, so that's what we'll focus on here.

Exercise: Accepting Yourself Fully—The Good, the Bad, and the Ugly

So, how do we begin the process of becoming whole within ourselves—not rejecting or casting away any aspect of ourselves but instead loving the whole picture? It's not as difficult as it sounds.

Of all the exercises and techniques I've described in this book, the one I'm about to present has taken me into deeper levels of connection through eye contact than I ever could have imagined. You can do this one alone.

Here's how it works:

1. Sit in a comfortable position on a chair, on a couch, or cross-legged on a cushion on the ground. Make sure you are in a quiet room, where you will not be disturbed for at least half an hour. Turn off all phones and ringers.

2. Start breathing with long, slow inhales and exhales, the

way we learned in Chapter 10. If you like, try the three-part breath described in that chapter.

3. Begin observing your thoughts and letting them pass without judgment, the way we did in Chapter 10.

4. Here's where the real power of this exercise comes in. When you've reached a state of relative calm and mental relaxation through the breathing and concentration, I want you to think of some aspect of yourself that you're not OK with—something that you frequently criticize, hide, or suppress.

If you're having trouble thinking of something at first, a good way to uncover these shadow aspects of yourself quickly is to complete one or more of the following sentences in your mind:

"Something about myself I'm not OK with is . . ."

"Something about myself I spend a lot of energy hiding is . . ."

"Something about myself I have trouble telling others is . . ."

We all have *something* that fits into these categories. Usually, it has to do with either something hurtful that someone else did to us, or something hurtful we did to someone else. Oftentimes, these feelings also center on body image and weight, or feelings of inadequacy or failure in our career or calling.

- Whatever it is, when you have found an aspect of your inner landscape that you're not OK with, sit with it. This is the practice. Let it sit there, hanging out in the open, without trying to hide it, suppress it, or will it away, and without judging it or criticizing it.

- Notice what physical sensations in your body go along with this thought. Let's say, for example, that you are not happy about your weight. If this is the case, you probably spend a lot of time criticizing yourself about your weight, beating yourself up about it, or trying to numb your mind to your unhappiness about the whole situation. But how often do you just sit and allow the thought and emotion— "I'm unhappy about my weight"—to be there, without piling on, interpreting it, hiding it, or forging some plan of action?

As soon as you just allow that thought to be there, or whatever the corresponding thought about your own situation is, you can begin to notice that the thought isn't just a thought, and it isn't just an emotion—it's also a body sensation: perhaps tingling, or tightness or constriction, or a feeling of energy charging throughout the body.

So, whatever the content of your thoughts or emotions, feel the body sensation that goes along with them. Let these sensations course through your body, your veins, your lungs, until you can really *feel what it feels like in your body* to hold these thoughts and emotions.

This may be the first time you've truly allowed this negative thought to sit in your body without trying to push it away or suppress it or ignore it. It may not be pleasant to do so—that's why you've pushed it away for so long. But stopping the pushing away and suppressing is precisely how you will learn to accept it, to accept all of you.

5. Here comes the heart of the practice. As you allow this abandoned emotion or thought to sit in your body, *send it love*. Recognize that it is a part of you, a part you have been pushing away or denying, and now you are accepting it. Now you are recognizing that this is as much a part of you as your hands and feet, your passions and joys, your hopes and aspirations.

    You may experience intense emotion as you send love to this previous castaway part of yourself. It may be the first time this aspect of you has been held in anything other than contempt and disregard. You may find a newfound energy and vitality coursing through you, now that you have relinquished the need to suppress a part of you.

6. One way we keep emotion suppressed and bottled up is by tensing our jaw and neck muscles. (We've already learned about this dynamic from Lance Mason in Chapter 4.) So, as you practice allowing yourself to feel emotions that you have previously held back, notice if there is any tension or clenching in your jaw area. Release this tension now. You may even find that opening your mouth and letting it hang slack helps in this regard. Yes, you look like a babbling fool when you do this—if someone were to see you. But fortunately you are alone, in private, so you don't need to pay any attention at all to how you look. Just pay attention to how you feel. Many people report that letting their jaw hang slack, releasing all the tension there, allows for previously suppressed emotion to come to the surface.

If you did this exercise, then you have just spent more time facing your hidden, suppressed, or abandoned parts of yourself than most people spend in a lifetime. You may experience a deeper sense of peace and self-acceptance.

As you walk around your life with this new capacity, notice when critical or self-judgmental thoughts come in. Practice self-acceptance of these thoughts as you go about your day—in line at the grocery store, on the bus or subway or in the car, as you walk on your lunch break, as you do the dishes.

Practice self-acceptance as you speak to others. Some of our most self-critical thoughts arise as we stand in the gaze of others—we imagine and project what they're thinking about us. As your capacity for self-acceptance grows, so will your capacity for clean, clear gaze with others.

It's no coincidence that the people I meet with the most steady, open, inviting gaze are usually people who have done the most amount of spiritual and emotional work to overcome their previous self-criticism and judgment about themselves—those who have come to the deepest state of self-acceptance.

Gazing at Number 1

We've talked about making eye contact with all kinds of people: complete strangers, sales prospects, audience members, co-workers, dates, friends, enemies, loved ones. There's only one person left we haven't talked about making eye contact with.

Yourself.

It's amazing how infrequently (if ever) we actually take the time to do this. As I pointed out in the introduction, the phrase "I want to be able to look him in the eye and say . . . " denotes the connection we make between truthfulness and direct eye contact. What about truthfulness with ourselves? When we are contemplating our own moral actions (or lack thereof), we often say something similar: "I want to be able to look myself in the mirror."

Given that we take this to be an intuitive, rock-bottom test of our own moral character and actions, how often do we actually look ourselves in the mirror? (At least, when our mouths aren't full of toothpaste during the morning rush?) I'm suggesting here that you actually take time to give yourself a good look, eye to eye.

Thus, I have one last exercise I'd like you to try. I'd like to close the book by having you try to make eye contact with the person you know best, yet have likely made the least eye contact with in your entire life.

The following is going to seem pretty far out to some

people. In fact, I may risk having some people dismiss me as loony. But I don't care, because I think this is a really powerful exercise.

Try eye gazing with yourself, in the mirror. If you can get over the seeming silliness of it, give this exercise a try. You might be surprised at what you find.

Obviously, you want to pick a place where no one else will see you. Doing this at a mirror in the middle of The Gap is not recommended—unless you'd like to accumulate a crowd of gawkers and be escorted out by security. I would also recommend against doing it in our normal place of self-reflection, the bathroom mirror! This can be quite an intense exercise, and I think it should be done in a slightly more reverential place. A chair in front of your bedroom mirror, when you are certain to be alone, is perfect. Adjust the lighting—not too bright, not too dark—as in other eye gazing exercises.

1. Begin gazing at yourself, just as you would gaze at a partner in the other eye gazing practices we've done.
2. You will almost certainly experience a raft of thoughts and emotions arising quickly. No one whom I'm aware of—certainly not me—enjoys a complete lack of self-judgment or self-criticism. Whatever negative thoughts about yourself that lurk around your depths will likely arise very quickly from this exercise. For women in particular, these judgments often center on physical appearance, age, weight, or body image with special ferocity. For both men and women, the judgments might focus on your accomplishments, station in life, achievements or perceived lack thereof, earnings, or other perceived failures in life. If you are one of the very few who jump immediately to thoughts and

feelings of self-love, appreciation, and acceptance during this exercise, congratulations; you have a lot to teach the rest of us, including me! More likely, though, you will experience at least *some* self-critical thoughts or emotions when looking at yourself.

3. Stay with these thoughts. As unpleasant as they may be, do not push them away, or add to them by being critical of yourself for having them, or even being critical of yourself for being critical of yourself for having them. ("Darn it! I'm not supposed to criticize myself for criticizing myself for having criticized myself!") Instead, bring the thoughts out of your head, where they can feel like an echo chamber or a dystopic funhouse, and into your body, by placing your awareness on what these thoughts *feel like* in your body. As we saw in the last exercise, almost every thought imaginable—particularly strong ones like the self-judgment we're examining—have a corresponding sensation in the body. I'm not talking about "feelings" in the sense of emotions—angry, sad, hurt, and so forth. I'm talking about actual physical sensation. If you pay close enough attention, you will notice that all these thoughts also go along with sensation in the body, which often feels like a tingling. I'm not exactly sure what this tingling is. Yogis would call it "prana" or "life force," and practitioners of t'ai chi would call it "chi." Because I'm trying to keep this book as accessible as possible to people of all spiritual faiths (and none), I'll just call it "sensation." All I know is that when I draw my attention way from the actual contents of the thoughts, I can definitely feel that thoughts have a corresponding sensation in the

body, and that focusing on the latter is a lot more calming than focusing on the former, which can be quite distressing.

4. Notice the amount of tension in your jaw and face. Often, tension in the jaw and face is so chronic, and we've become so habituated to it, that we don't even notice it. Release the tension in your face. Once you are secure in the knowledge that no one is looking at you or judging you, you might be shocked to discover that what comes up—when you finally allow yourself to relax your facial muscles—is a look of tiredness, or even sadness. Many of us are truly exhausted by the social demands of having to pretend we're happy and cheerful around the clock—particularly during the workday. Allow whatever arises to arise. Allow it to be there. Practice the same open, loving, accepting gaze toward yourself and all that is within you that we've been practicing in this book toward others.

You deserve it.

Epilogue

Several months before my deadline for this book, I was told I had a tumor on my left testicle, with a 97 percent chance it was cancer.

Four days after I heard a second opinion confirming this judgment, I was on an operating table at Memorial Sloan-Kettering Cancer Center in Manhattan, about to receive general anesthesia to have one of my two favorite spherical appendages removed.

As someone who has taken writing seriously since my teens, I have written all kinds of things that, in the hindsight of months or years, seemed frivolous, trivial, or irrelevant.

One of my strongest tests for deciding if a piece of writing I've produced has lasting value to me and others is whether it seems worthwhile or useful, not just when all is rosy but also when life throws me its challenges and hurdles.

When Jena first walked into the recovery area after my surgery, I caught her eyes. They were full of compassion, love, warmth, nurturing, and human embrace. That one glance, in less than a second, set me at ease in a frightening and vulnerable time. I knew I would be OK.

My publisher graciously offered me extra time to complete this book. It certainly would make sense to slow down on a book project when one gets diagnosed with cancer (Stage I seminoma, it turned out. Fortunately, it has not yet spread, and I am under wonderful care.)

Yet in that fraction-of-a-second glance into Jena's eyes right after the surgery, not only did I know I would be OK, I also knew I was writing about something important and valuable for others. I was determined to make the deadline, and I did.

May you experience a gaze as loving, deep, and embracing as the one I had the joy of experiencing in that moment.

That is my wish for you.

Acknowledgments

I owe a deep debt of gratitude, and offer my sincere thanks, to James Baraz, author of *Awakening Joy,* who was kind enough to connect a young, unproven author to his literary agent.

Stephanie Tade, the wonderful agent to whom James connected me. Stephanie, you believed in this project from the start and worked hard on it. I will always be grateful.

Peter Hubbard, who showed my proposal to just the right people at HarperCollins. You played a huge part in helping me realize my lifelong dream: to become a published author.

Michael Signorelli, my editor at Harper Perennial. I don't know how many authors can use the word "fun" to describe their experience working with their editor, but I am one of the lucky ones. Beyond that, your input, feedback, and guidance were invaluable and left a huge mark on this book.

Jena la Flamme, Annie Lalla, and my parents also gave me incisive, excellent, and extensive editorial feedback on the first draft, which made this a much better book.

Cal Morgan and Carrie Kania, other members of the Harper Perennial team, who believed in me and gave me a shot.

Thomas Farber, novelist, my writing mentor since Day One. We started out bartering my salsa instruction for his editing of my writing, hour for hour, even as he was billing others at a rate five times my salsa rate. We have since become great friends, and his salsa is pretty darn good now, too. Tom, you've always been there for me, and I can't tell you how much it means to me.

Margaret Gee, an Australian literary agent I met at a San Francisco dinner party four years ago, who helped get me into this mad, mad world of publishing, and who encouraged me and mentored me all along the way. I couldn't have done this without you.

All those who helped me get Eye Gazing Parties off the ground, even when it was just a crazy idea in my head: Max Track, Jaimal Yogis, Ariana Green, Solaria Perez-Stepanov, Amy McCloskey, Destin Gerek (aka The Erotic Rockstar), and Neo Young.

All the people who were kind enough to offer me extensive interviews. They all responded to an e-mail about eye contact, many of them barely knowing a thing about me, taking a chance that it would be worth their while: Karl Albrecht, Steve Albrecht, Tony Alessandra, Chris Attwood, Nancy Bardacke, Coleman Barks, Sera Beak, Nicholas Boothman, Nick Bollettieri, David Brooks, Victor Cheng, Garrison Cohen, Diane DiResta, Bert Decker, Quentin English, Frans de Waal, Paul Ekman, Urijah Faber, Debra Fine, Helen Fisher, Marie Forleo, Lauren Frances, Matt Furey, Sharon Gannon, Lee Glickstein, Leslie Handmacher, Gay and Kathlyn Hendricks, Nancy Jaicks, Will Johnson, Darren LaCroix, Jay Conrad Levinson, Jeanne Martinet, Steve Marx, Lance Mason, Jess McCann, Steve McCurry, Ivan Misner, Michael Murphy, Michael Notaro, Matt Oechsli, Judith Orloff, Lou Paget, Zan Perrion, Paul Powers, Neil Rackham, Peter Shankman, Janis Spindel, Sean Stephenson, Ed Tate, Regena Thomashauer (aka Mama Gena), Mark Wiskup, David Wood, and Victoria Zdrok. Your input literally made this book.

Thanks also to Sandor Gardos, Liyana Silver, Michael

Notaro, Tom Farber, James Baraz, Stephanie Tade, Adam Gilad, and Jaimal Yogis for connecting me to some of my interviewees.

My parents, Daniel and Patricia Ellsberg, for never giving up on believing in me, not for a second. I will always love you.

Jena la Flamme. My best friend, co-conspirator, life partner, salsa diva, nutritional mentor, eye gazing consort, and love of my life. I can't even begin to express the gratitude I feel every day for having you in my life.

Ralph Waldo Emerson on Eyes and Eye Contact:

From *The Conduct of Life* (1860)

One of the most eloquent, insightful, and extensive pieces of writing I've encountered on the psychological power of eyes and eye contact comes from Ralph Waldo Emerson, in his published lectures, *The Conduct of Life*.

A main fact in the history of manners is the wonderful expressiveness of the human body. If it were made of glass, or of air, and the thoughts were written on steel tablets within, it could not publish more truly its meaning than now. Wise men read very sharply all your private history in your look and gait and behavior. The whole economy of nature is bent on expression. The tell-tale body is all tongues. Men are like Geneva watches with crystal faces which expose the whole movement. They carry the liquor of life flowing up and

down in these beautiful bottles, and announcing to the curious how it is with them. The face and eyes reveal what the
spirit is doing, how old it is, what aims it has. The eyes indicate the antiquity of the soul, or, through how many forms it
has already ascended. It almost violates the proprieties, if we
say above the breath here, what the confessing eyes do not
hesitate to utter to every street passenger.

Man cannot fix his eye on the sun, and so far seems
imperfect. In Siberia, a late traveller found men who could
see the satellites of Jupiter with their unarmed eye. In some
respects the animals excel us. The birds have a longer sight,
beside the advantage by their wings of a higher observa-
tory. A cow can bid her calf, by secret signal, probably of
the eye, to run away, or to lie down and hide itself. The
jockeys say of certain horses, that "they look over the whole
ground." The out-door life, and hunting, and labor, give
equal vigor to the human eye. A farmer looks out at you
as strong as the horse; his eye-beam is like the stroke of a
staff. An eye can threaten like a loaded and levelled gun, or
can insult like hissing or kicking; or, in its altered mood, by
beams of kindness, it can make the heart dance with joy.

The eye obeys exactly the action of the mind. When
a thought strikes us, the eyes fix, and remain gazing at
a distance; in enumerating the names of persons or of
countries, as France, Germany, Spain, Turkey, the eyes
wink at each new name. There is no nicety of learning
sought by the mind, which the eyes do not vie in acquir-
ing. "An artist," said Michel Angelo, "must have his mea-
suring tools not in the hand, but in the eye;" and there is
no end to the catalogue of its performances, whether in
indolent vision, (that of health and beauty,) or in strained
vision, (that of art and labor).

Eyes are bold as lions,—roving, running, leaping, here

and there, far and near. They speak all languages. They
wait for no introduction; they are no Englishmen; ask
no leave of age, or rank; they respect neither poverty nor
riches, neither learning nor power, nor virtue, nor sex, but
intrude, and come again, and go through and through you,
in a moment of time. What inundation of life and thought
is discharged from one soul into another, through them!
The glance is natural magic. The mysterious communication established across a house between two entire strangers, moves all the springs of wonder. The communication
by the glance is in the greatest part not subject to the control of the will. It is the bodily symbol of identity of nature.
We look into the eyes to know if this other form is another
self, and the eyes will not lie, but make a faithful confession
what inhabitant is there. The revelations are sometimes ter-
rific. The confession of a low, usurping devil is there made,
and the observer shall seem to feel the stirring of owls, and
bats, and horned hoofs, where he looked for innocence and
simplicity. 'Tis remarkable, too, that the spirit that appears
at the windows of the house does at once invest himself in
a new form of his own, to the mind of the beholder.

The eyes of men converse as much as their tongues, with
the advantage, that the ocular dialect needs no dictionary,
but is understood all the world over. When the eyes say
one thing, and the tongue another, a practised man relies
on the language of the first. If the man is off his centre, the
eyes show it. You can read in the eyes of your companion,
whether your argument hits him, though his tongue will
not confess it. There is a look by which a man shows he is
going to say a good thing, and a look when he has said it.
Vain and forgotten are all the fine offers and offices of hos-
pitality, if there is no holiday in the eye. How many furtive
inclinations avowed by the eye, though dissembled by the

lips! One comes away from a company, in which, it may easily happen, he has said nothing, and no important remark has been addressed to him, and yet, if in sympathy with the society, he shall not have a sense of this fact, such a stream of life has been flowing into him, and out from him, through the eyes. There are eyes, to be sure, that give no more admission into the man than blueberries. Others are liquid and deep,— wells that a man might fall into;—others are aggressive and devouring, seem to call out the police, take all too much notice, and require crowded Broadways, and the security of millions, to protect individuals against them. The military eye I meet, now darkly sparkling under clerical, now under rustic brows. 'Tis the city of Lacedaemon; 'tis a stack of bayonets. There are asking eyes, asserting eyes, prowling eyes; and eyes full of fate,—some of good, and some of sinister omen. The alleged power to charm down insanity, or ferocity in beasts, is a power behind the eye. It must be a victory achieved in the will, before it can be signified in the eye. 'Tis very certain that each man carries in his eye the exact indication of his rank in the immense scale of men, and we are always learning to read it. A complete man should need no auxiliaries to his personal presence. Whoever looked on him would consent to his will, being certified that his aims were generous and universal. The reason why men do not obey us, is because they see the mud at the bottom of our eye. . . .

Balzac left in manuscript a chapter, which he called "Theorie de la demarche," in which he says: "The look, the voice, the respiration, and the attitude or walk, are identical. But, as it has not been given to man, the power to stand guard, at once, over these four different simultaneous expressions of his thought, watch that one which speaks out the truth, and you will know the whole man."

Notes

Epigraph

1. Cervantes, 101. Tr. by the author.

A Note to Readers

1. It is well-known, for example, that norms around personal space and physical contact during conversations (hugging, touching the arms, etc.) differ from culture to culture. (The definitive book on this topic is *The Silent Language* by Edward Hall.) I have traveled extensively in Latin America, and some of the sheer physical closeness and physical touch I've experienced in conversation, even from men, would make many gringos feel very uncomfortable.

    While I was writing this book I heard many different things about the relation between eye contact and race or culture. I heard that Japanese people are trained to look you in the neck and not the eyes during conversation. One online article claimed that this purported trait was "a holdover from Samurai days, when peasants risked decapitation by looking a samurai in the eye" (www.onpedia.com/encyclopedia/eye-contact, accessed January 2, 2009). I heard that Latin Americans don't make direct eye contact with people of higher status; I heard that, while whites tend to avoid eye contact while speaking and make eye contact while listening, blacks do the opposite, which is supposedly the source of many miscommunications between the races. I even heard that Native Americans do not need to make direct eye contact because they already always "feel oneness" with whomever they're speaking with, so eye contact for them is superfluous.

While I have no doubt that there are cultural differences and customs concerning the appropriateness and use of eye contact, I was unable to find any serious scientific studies on the subject or in fact anything that went beyond random and unsubstantiated anecdotes.

I offer this observation on this topic, however: While I am sure there are cultures in which eye contact is frowned upon in conversation, I am not aware of any culture that fails to recognize the power of eyes and eye contact. Those cultures that discourage eye contact in social interaction, it seems, do so precisely out of a recognition for how powerful and potentially unsettling a gaze can be. That recognition is universal.

The main advice I offer for those navigating the waters of eye contact in cross-cultural settings is a refrain I will repeat throughout this book: eye contact is a dance. It involves two willing partners. If you are the only willing partner, that is called staring, and I can guarantee you that no one, no matter what culture, country, or race they come from, likes the feeling of being stared at. (More on this in Chapter 1.)

So, if you're talking with someone who—for whatever reason, cultural or personal—does not feel comfortable with eye contact, it does little good to ram it down their eyes in the name of connecting with them or projecting confidence. Each of us has our own comfort zone regarding how much eye contact feels right to us. My aim in this book is to help anyone who would like to expand that comfort zone and to improve the quality of eye contact within it.

Introduction

1. www.quotationspage.com/quotes/Cicero (cited 7 Feb. 2009).
2. Matthew 6:22-23 NASB.
3. Jerome, 106.
4. Shakespeare, *Love's Labour's Lost*, IV, iii, 330.

5. qt. in Zdrok, 108.
6. Whitman.
7. See Appendix.

Chapter 1: What Bill Clinton Knows About Eye Contact

1. Applebome.
2. Wenn.com, "Anderson Swept Away by Clinton." Quoted in www.imdb.com/news/ni0269074/ (accessed April 10, 2009).
3. Goleman, 38.
4. For a more in-depth account of this academic back-and-forth, told from Ekman's perspective, see his introduction to the 1998 edition of Darwin's *The Expression of the Emotions in Man and Animals* (Oxford UP).
5. Darwin, 28.
6. Darwin, 270–271.
7. Darwin, 240.
8. Fast, 122.
9. For a fascinating discussion of the evolution of the whites of the eyes in humans and its implications for our understanding of human social dynamics, published in—of all places—the op-ed page of the *New York Times*, see Tomasello.
10. Darwin, 204.
11. Beak, xxvii.
12. Quoted in www.brainyquote.com/quotes/keywords/battlefield.html (accessed October 21, 2009).
13. Gladwell, 194–195.
14. Goleman, 11.
15. Elkins, 162, 168.
16. Goleman, 42.
17. Goleman, 86, 87.
18. Goleman, 87.
19. Goleman 91, 40, 43
20. Goleman, 63–64.
21. Schnarch, 212.
22. See, for example, Stanbury.
23. González-Crussi, 114–115.

Chapter 2: How to Become a Master of Eye Contact in Two Weeks

1. See Hall, *The Hidden Dimension*.
2. Csikszentmihalyi, 28.

Chapter 3: Eye Flirting, Part I

1. Thackeray.
2. McCann, locations 617–19.
3. McCann, locations 657–62.
4. Fein and Schneider, locations 265, 457–461.
5. Yara.
6. Forleo, 71.
7. Behrendt and Tuccillo, 44.

Chapter 4: Eye Flirting, Part II

1. Zdrok, 100.
2. Zdrok, 108.
3. Kuhnke, 100.
4. Slater.
5. Slater.
6. Brunstein.

Chapter 5: The Eyes Are the Windows to the Sale

1. Decker, 114-115.
2. Decker, 115.
3. Stephenson, 42.
4. Tracy and Arden, 42.
5. Bliss, "Customer Bliss," 2.

Chapter 6: How to Wow a Crowd with Eye Contact

1. Glickstein, 100–101.

Chapter 7: If Looks Could Kill

1. Attributed to "Pierce Butler, Natchez, Mississippi" on www
   .rulesofthumb.org. There are many Pierce Butlers throughout
   history, but only one that I could find—James Pierce Butler—
   was from Natchez, Mississippi. He was a banker who played a
   controversial role in efforts to protect New Orleans from the
   Great Mississippi River Flood of 1927. If you have any better
   information about the origins of this quote, please contact me
   at Michael@powerofeyecontact.com.
2. Shakespeare, *As You Like It*, III, v, 1661.
3. González-Crussi, 100.
4. See Appendix.

Chapter 8: Truth and Eyes

1. quoted in www.quotationpark.com/topics/eye.html (accessed
   April 12, 2009).
2. www.bbc.co.uk/dna/h2g2/A48400463 (accessed
   October 21, 2009).
3. Fitzpatrick.
4. www.time.com/time/magazine/article/
   0,9171,925882,00.html (accessed October 21, 2009).
5. quoted in Ibid.
6. www.bbc.co.uk/dna/h2g2/A48400463 (accessed
   October 21, 2009).
7. Ellsberg, 43.
8. Dalai Lama and Ekman, 37.
9. Hare, 10.
10. Ekman, "Why Don't We Catch Liars?"
11. Eliot.

Chapter 9: Eye Love You

1. Montaigne, 403.
2. Shakespeare, *Romeo and Juliet*, II, ii, 858–867.
3. Shakespeare, Sonnet XVII.

4. Spenser.
5. Kurson, 278.

Chapter 10: Gazing at the Divine

1. Previously titled *Rumi: Gazing at the Beloved: The Radical Practice of Beholding the Divine.*
2. Johnson, 18.
3. Johnson, 21.
4. Johnson, 29–30.
5. Rumi, 12.
6. See Appendix.
7. Csikszentmihalyi, 119.
8. Benson, 10.

Works Cited

Applebome, Peter. "Bill Clinton's Uncertain Journey." *New York Times Magazine,* March 8, 1992.

Beak, Sera. *The Red Book: A Deliciously Unorthodox Approach to Igniting Your Divine Spark.* New York: Jossey-Bass, 2006.

Behrendt, Greg and Liz Tuccillo. *He's Just Not That Into You: The No-Excuse Truth to Understanding Guys.* New York: Simon Spotlight Entertainment, 2004.

Benson, Herbert. *The Relaxation Response.* New York: Harper-Torch, 2000.

Bliss, Jeanne. *Chief Customer Officer: Getting Past Lip Service to Passionate Action.* New York: Jossey-Bass, 2006.

———. "Customer Bliss: Do Your Customers Love You?" *Sales and Service Excellence,* June 2006, 6:6.

Brunstein, Ada. "Eye to I."web.mit.edu/sciwrite/news/thesisexcerpts07.html#brunstein (accessed June 13, 2009).

Cervantes, Miguel de. *Don Quijote de la Mancha.* Madrid: Espasa, 1998.

Csikszentmihalyi, Mihaly. *Flow: The Psychology of Optimal Experience.* New York: Harper Perennial, 2008.

Dalai Lama and Paul Ekman. *Emotional Awareness: Overcoming the Obstacles to Psychological Balance and Compassion: A Conversation*

Between the Dalai Lama and Paul Ekman, Ph.D. Ed. Paul Ekman. New York: Times Books, 2008.

Darwin, Charles. *The Expression of the Emotions in Man and Animals.* Chicago: University of Chicago Press, 1965.

Decker, Bert. *You've Got to Be Believed to Be Heard: The Complete Book of Speaking . . . in Business and in Life.* New York: St. Martin's, 2008.

DiResta, Diane. *Knockout Presentations: How to Deliver Your Message with Power, Punch and Pizzaz.* Worcester, MA: Chandler House Press, 1998.

Ekman, Paul. "Why Don't We Catch Liars?" *Social Research,* Fall 1996, 801–817.

Eliot, George. *The Mill on the Floss.* www.gutenberg.org/dirs/etext04/mlfls10h.htm (accessed April 12, 2009).

Elkins, James. *The Object Stares Back: On the Nature of Seeing.* New York: Harcourt, 1996.

Ellsberg, Daniel. *Secrets: A Memoir of Vietnam and the Pentagon Papers.* New York: Viking, 2002.

Emerson, Ralph Waldo. *The Conduct of Life.* www.rwe.org/works/Conduct_5_Behavior.htm (accessed April 11, 2009).

Fast, Julius. *Body Language.* 2nd ed. New York: MJF Books, 2002.

Fein, Ellen, and Sherrie Schneider. *All The Rules: Time-Tested Secrets for Capturing the Heart of Mr. Right.* Kindle edition. New York: Grand Central, 2008.

Fitzpatrick, Tom. "The Lover." www.phoenixnewtimes.com/1991-02-06/news/the-lover (accessed October 21, 2009).

Forleo, Marie. *Make Every Man Want You: How to Be So Irresistible You'll Barely Keep from Dating Yourself.* New York: McGraw-Hill, 2008.

Gladwell, Malcolm. *Blink: The Power of Thinking Without Thinking.* New York: Back Bay Books, 2007.

Glickstein, Lee. *Be Heard Now! Tap Into Your Inner Speaker and Communicate with Ease.* New York: Broadway Books, 1998.

Goleman, Daniel. *Social Intelligence: The Revolutionary New Science of Human Relationships*. New York: Bantam Dell, 2006.

González-Crussi, F. *On Seeing: Things Seen, Unseen, and Obscene*. New York: Overlook Duckworth, 2006.

Hall, Edward T. *The Hidden Dimension*. New York: Anchor, 1966.

————. *The Silent Language*. New York: Anchor, 1973.

Hare, Robert D. *Without Conscience: The Disturbing World of the Psychopaths Among Us*. New York: Guilford Press, 1999.

Jerome. *Nicene and Post-Nicene Fathers, Second Series, Volume VI*. Ed. Philip Schaff and Henry Wallace. New York: Cosimo, 2007.

Johnson, Will. *Rumi: Gazing at the Beloved: The Radical Practice of Beholding the Divine*. Rochester, VT: Inner Traditions, 2003.

Kuhnke, Elizabeth. *Body Language for Dummies*. Chichester, West Sussex, England: Wiley, 2007.

Kurson, Robert. *Crashing Through: The Extraordinary True Story of the Man Who Dared to See*. New York: Random House, 2007.

McCann, Jess. *You Lost Him at Hello: A Saleswoman's Secrets to Closing the Deal with Any Guy You Want*. Kindle edition. Deerfield Beach, FL: HCI, 2008.

Montaigne, Michel de. *Complete Works*. Ed. and Tr. Donald Murdoch Frame. New York: Knopf, 2003.

Murphy, Michael. *The Future of the Body: Explorations into the Future Evolution of Human Nature*. New York: Tarcher, 2003.

Powers, Paul. *Winning Job Interviews: Reduce Interview Anxiety, Outprepare the Other Candidates, and Land the Job You Love*. Franklin Lakes, NJ: Career Press, 2004.

Rumi, Jalal al-Din. *The Glance: Songs of Soul-Meeting*. Tr. Coleman Barks. New York: Viking Arkana, 1999.

Schnarch, David. *Passionate Marriage: Keeping Love and Intimacy Alive in Committed Relationships*. New York: Holt Paperbacks, 1998.

Shakespeare, William. *As You Like It*. www.opensourceshakespeare .org/views/plays/playmenu.php?WorkID=asyoulikeit (accessed April 11, 2009).

————. *Love's Labour's Lost.* www.opensourceshakespeare.org/ views/plays/play_view.php?WorkID=loveslabours&Scope=entire &pleasewait=1&msg=pl (accessed April 11, 2009).

————. *Romeo and Juliet.* www.opensourceshakespeare.org/views/ plays/play_view.php?WorkID=romeojuliet&Scope=entire&pleasewait =1&msg=pl (accessed April 12, 2009).

————. Sonnet XVII. www.opensourceshakespeare.org/views/ sonnets/sonnet_view.php?Sonnet=17 (accessed April 12, 2009).

Slater, Lauren. "True Love." http://ngm.nationalgeographic .com/2006/02/true-love/slater-text/10 (accessed June 13, 2009).

Spenser, Edmund. "Amoretti." www.theotherpages.org/poems/ spenser1.html (accessed April 12, 2009).

Stanbury, Sarah. "The Lover's Gaze in Troilus and Criseyde." *Chaucer's Troilus and Criseyde: Essays in Criticism.* Ed. Richard Allen Shoaf and Catherine S. Cox. Tempe, Ariz: Medieval & Renaissance Texts & Studies, 1992.

Stephenson, Sean. *Get Off Your "But": How to End Self-Sabotage and Stand Up for Yourself.* New York: Jossey-Bass, 2009.

Strauss, Neil. *The Game: Penetrating the Secret Society of Pickup Artists.* New York: William Morrow, 2005.

Thackeray, William Makepeace. *The History of Henry Esmond, Esq.* www.gutenberg.org/files/2511/2511-h/2511-h.htm (accessed April 14, 2009).

Tomasello, Michael. "For Human Eyes Only." www.nytimes.com/ 2007/01/13/opinion/13tomasello.html?scp=1&sq=evolution%20 of%20whites%20of%20eyes&st=cse (accesssed June 16, 2009).

Tracy, Brian, and Ron Arden. *The Power of Charm: How to Win Anyone Over in Any Situation.* New York: AMACOM, 2006.

Whitman, Walt. "Song of Myself." *Leaves of Grass.* www .princeton.edu/~batke/logr/log_026.html (accessed June 13, 2009).

Wiskup, Mark. *The It Factor: Be the One People Like, Listen to, and Remember.* New York: AMACOM, 2007.

Yara, Susan. "Life Coaching to Lose Weight." www.forbes.com/2006/05/25/life-coaching-fitness_cx_sy_0530htow.html (accessed June 16, 2009).

Zdrok, Victoria. *Dr. Z on Scoring: How to Pick Up, Seduce, and Hook Up with Hot Women.* New York: Fireside, 2008.

Interviewees

Tony Alessandra is a prolific author of sales books, including the sales classics *Non-Manipulative Selling* and *Collaborative Selling*. He has conducted sales trainings for hundreds of major corporations and trade associations in dozens of industries. (www.alessandra.com)

Chris Attwood is the author, with Janet Bray Attwood, of the bestseller *The Passion Test: The Effortless Path to Discovering Your Destiny.* (www.thepassiontest.com) Chris and Janet also publish the online personal development magazine www.HealthyWealthNWise.com.

Coleman Barks is widely considered the preeminent translator of Rumi into English. He is the bestselling author of *The Essential Rumi, The Soul of Rumi,* and *Rumi: The Book of Love.* (www.colemanbarks.com)

Sera Beak is a "world-traveled, Harvard-trained scholar of mysticism and comparative religion and an intrepid spiritual cowgirl," as described on the back cover of her book, *The Red Book: A Deliciously Unorthodox Approach to Igniting Your Divine Spark.* (www.serabeak.com)

Jeanne Bliss is author of *Chief Customer Officer: Getting Past Lip Service to Passionate Action.* She has been known as the "Chief Customer Zealot" for five major corporations. She was the leader of the Lands' End Customer Experience and the Officer for Customer Satisfaction & Retention at Allstate. She also served as Microsoft General Manager of Worldwide Customer & Partner Loyalty and as Senior Manager for Customer Satisfaction at Mazda. (www.customerbliss.com)

Nick Bollettieri is a legendary tennis coach. He has personally coached nine players ranked number one in the world: Andre Agassi, Boris Becker, Jim Courier, Martina Hingis, Marcelo Rios, Monica Seles, Venus Williams, Serena Williams, and Maria Sharapova. He is the founder of IMG Academies in Florida, elite sports training schools. (www. imgacademies.com)

David Brooks is the 1990 Toastmasters World Champion of Public Speaking. He is a speaking trainer who has taught over 100,000 business professionals how to improve their public speaking and communication. (www.davidbrookstexas.com)

Victor Cheng is one of the nation's leading experts in growing a business during a recession. He is the author of *The Recession-Proof Business: Lessons from the Greatest Recession Success Stories of All Time* and has appeared on Fox News, MSNBC, and in the *Wall Street Journal*. He has lectured at the Harvard Business School. Previously he was a consultant at McKinsey & Company. (www.victorcheng.com)

Frans de Waal, Ph.D., is one of the most widely cited primatologists in the world. He is a professor of primate behavior at Emory University and the author of many books, including *Our Inner Ape: A Leading Primatologist Explains Why We Are Who We Are* and *Chimpanzee Politics: Power and Sex Among Apes*.

Diane DiResta is the author of *Knockout Presentations: How to Deliver Your Message With Power, Punch and Pizzazz*. She is a communications coach whose client list includes AT&T, Chase, IBM, Reuters, IBM, and the NBA. She has been cited in the *Wall Street Journal* and the *New York Times*. (www.diresta.com)

Paul Ekman, Ph.D., is professor emeritus of psychology at the University of California, San Francisco. He is the leading expert on the expression of emotions through the face. He is the author of fourteen books, including *Emotional Awareness: Overcoming the Obstacles to Psychological Balance and Compassion*, co-authored with the Dalai Lama. (www.paulekman.com)

Urijah Faber is one of the most popular mixed martial arts champions in the world. He has held world title belts in the World Extreme Cagefighting, King of the Cage, and Gladiator Challenge leagues. (www.urijahfaber.com)

Lauren Frances is a Los Angeles–based dating coach who leads workshops all over the world for women on how to be more effective in flirting and dating. She is the author of *Dating, Mating and Manhandling: An Ornithological Guide to Men*. (www.laurenfrances.com)

Matt Furey is the author of *Combat Conditioning* and is one of the top trainers of "functional fitness" conditioning for martial artists in the world (strength training using body weight and naturalistic movements rather than weights). A national champion wrestler in college, in 1997 Furey became the first non-Chinese person to win the world championship of Shuai-Chiao, a form of kung fu, in Beijing. He is the author of a very popular fitness newsletter online. (www.mattfurey.com)

Lee Glickstein is the author of *Be Heard Now! Tap Into Your Inner Speaker and Communicate with Ease* and the founder of Speaking Circles, an international speaker training organization. (www.speakingcircles.com)

Gay Hendricks, Ph.D., and Kathlyn Hendricks, Ph.D., are two of the most widely respected teachers in the world on intimacy and inspired relationships. They lead workshops on these and other topics around the world. They are the authors of numerous books, including *Conscious Loving: The Journey to Co-Commitment*. (www.hendricks.com)

Will Johnson is the author of *The Spiritual Practices of Rumi: Radical Techniques for Beholding the Divine* and numerous other books on spiritual topics. (www.embodiment.net)

Darren LaCroix is the 2001 Toastmasters World Champion of Public Speaking. He now travels the globe as a successful keynote speaker. (www.DarrenLaCroix.com)

Annie Lalla is a relationships coach based in New York City. She writes and edits a web magazine called Wonder "for the emotionally astute female intellectual." (www.wonderzine. net)

Jess McCann parlayed her success in the sales profession into dating success and wrote the book *You Lost Him at Hello: A Saleswoman's Secrets to Closing the Deal with Any Guy You Want.* She is now a full-time dating coach. (www.jessmc-cann.com)

Steve McCurry is the photographer of "Afghan Girl," the famous cover of the June 1985 issue of *National Geographic.* (www.stevemccurry.com)

Ivan Misner, Ph.D., is the founder of Business Network International, the largest business networking organization in the world. BNI has 5,400 chapters around the globe and is responsible for $2.3 billion of referral business for its members each year. He is the author of the *New York Times* bestsellers *Truth or Delusion?: Busting Networking's Biggest Myths* and *Masters of Networking: Building Relationships for Your Pocketbook and Soul* and is widely cited as "the father of modern networking." (www.bni.com)

Michael Murphy is the founder of the Esalen Institute in Big Sur, California, which was an epicenter for the development of transpersonal and humanistic psychology, and the human potential movement in general, in the sixties and seventies. Murphy played a central role in founding these fields. (www.esalen.org)

Paul Powers, Ph.D., is a management psychologist who has been featured in the *Wall Street Journal* and on CNN, MSNBC, and NPR. He is the author of *Winning Job Interviews: Reduce Interview Anxiety, Outprepare the Other Candidates, and Land the Job You Love*, one of the top-ranking job interview books on Amazon. (www.drpaulpowers.com)

Neil Rackham is the author of the legendary sales book *SPIN Selling*, one of the only sales books ever to be based on large-scale, in-field observation of tens of thousands of sales calls. (www.neilrackham.com)

Janis Spindel is one of the world's most upscale matchmakers. Her male clients pay her up to $500,000 to find their match. She has been featured on *Dr. Phil*, the *Today* show, and CNN; in the *New Yorker;* and numerous times in the *New York Times*. She is responsible for over nine hundred marriages. She is the author of *How to Date Men: Dating Secret's from America's Top Matchmaker*. (www.janisspindel matchmaker.com)

Ed Tate is the 2000 Toastmasters World Champion of Public Speaking. He is a keynote speaker and a speaking and sales trainer. (www.edtate.com)

Regena Thomashauer, aka Mama Gena, teaches popular workshops for women on how to "use the power of pleasure to have their way with the world." She is the author of the bestselling *Mama Gena's School of Womanly Arts* and several other books, and she has been featured on the *Today Show, 20/20*, and NPR and in the *New York Times*. (www.mamagenas.com)

Mark Wiskup is a communications coach who has consulted across a wide range of industries, including for many Fortune 500 companies. He is the author of *The It Factor: Be the One People Like, Listen to, and Remember*. (www.wiskup communications.com)

Free Bonus Material for Readers of

The Power of Eye Contact

For free extras to this book, including access to a teleseminar series covering the topics discussed here, audio interviews with experts, the ebooks "How to Host an Eye Gazing Party" and "Beauty Secrets for Better Eye Contact," and a free subscription to the "Power of Eye Contact" newsletter with stories, tips, and insights that go beyond what could fit into this book, visit www.powerofeyecontact.com/bonus.